CHILDREN'S LAST DAYS

*To the beloved memories of Róisín (1972–1985)
and all the children whose last days are here
remembered*

Children's Last Days

by
ANNA FARMAR

Town House

Published in 1992 by
Town House
42 Morehampton Road
Donnybrook
Dublin 4

© Anna Farmar 1992

All rights reserved. No part of this publication may be reproduced, stored in a retrieval system, or transmitted in any form or by any means, electronic, mechanical, photocopying, recording or otherwise, without the prior permission of the publishers.

British Library Cataloguing in Publication Data available

ISBN: 0-948524-42-1

Typeset by Printset & Design Ltd, Dublin
Printed in Ireland by Criterion Press, Dublin

Contents

Preface 7

Acknowledgements 10

Chapter 1 Cancer and children 11

Chapter 2 The bombshell 16

Chapter 3 An uncertain future 23

Chapter 4 Getting information, making decisions 30

Chapter 5 Looking for kindness 42

Chapter 6 Cancer in the family 59

Chapter 7 Support from the community 73

Chapter 8 Terminal care 85

Chapter 9 Pain 99

Chapter 10 Last days 117

Chapter 11 Grief 128

Appendix: Details of sample and method 138

Notes and references 149

Bibliography 153

Index 166

Surely goodness and kindness shall follow me
   All the days of my life

Psalm 23

Preface

Our daughter Róisín was two and a half years old when she contracted leukaemia. She lived for another ten years — years of 'normal' living, recorded in many happy family photographs, with the smiling child, the very picture of health, beaming at the camera.

But the good times were punctuated with crises when the disease recurred and Rosie had to endure the painful, debilitating treatment which prolonged her life and held out the hope of cure. Chemotherapy made her sick, steroids puffed out her face, gave her a ravenous appetite, and bloated her body. Her hair fell out; at two and a half she didn't mind, and like other little bald children she would imitate us and brush her hairless head. But when she relapsed at seven and again at nine years old, and even worse when she relapsed for the last time when she was on the verge of adolescence, the thinning hair and the puffiness from steroids were hard for her to bear.

These were the side-effects; the administration of the treatment was a trial in itself: the endless needles, the painful bone-marrow tests, the injections into her spine, the local anaesthetics that entailed yet more injections, and never seemed quite to deaden the pain. She was always stoical but her endurance was worn down over the years.

When she was very low she cried desperately: 'Why me? Why does it have to be me?' On a sunny afternoon when she was about seven, weak and feverish, she lay in bed to the sound of her brother and his friends larking in the garden below her bedroom window. She sighed: 'They're all having fun and I'm not.' It was true and there was no answer to her question.

She was very ill the Christmas before she died. Delirious for days on end, she called for me, biting her fingernails till they bled, but she could not hear me, though I held her and told her I was with her. That was one of the worst times. She came out of that crisis and recovered to a degree, but while still in hospital the pain in her bones broke through. She screamed with fear and pain and the ward sister ran for the morphine. When the drug had taken effect, a young nurse helped her to sit up and began to wash her. Rosie, a little high from the morphine, smiled drowsily and remarked, looking down at her thin legs: 'This poor body has suffered so much.' 'Oh, don't say that,' protested the young nurse. But Rosie insisted: 'Well, it has.'

In due course, Róisín's doctor gently told us that we had come to the end of active treatment. From here on, medication would be aimed at controlling symptoms, not at curing the disease or keeping her alive. She might live for a year or eighteen months.

In some ways this clarity was a relief. No more would Róisín have to endure the bone-marrow and blood tests. The roller-coaster of hopes raised and dashed, the strain of uncertainty, the possibility of cure, of advances in treatment tantalisingly held out, the fear of what the drugs were doing to her, of what the future held; these were over. At least now we could concentrate on keeping her comfortable, and making her and our last days together as content as possible.

Róisín's last days were indeed full of peace, but they were preceded by weeks of crises, of panic-stricken dashes to hospital when her pain leapt out of control, of times of fear and near-despair. We did not get the help we needed until late in her terminal illness. The shock of that lack remains with me still.

From the moment of her diagnosis, in London in 1975, Róisín had received the best of care. She had attended one of the most famous hospitals in the world, with its team of specialists in cancer care, and on our return to live in Dublin had been referred to another outstanding specialist. We had never had to worry about the costs of such advanced treatment, or the expensive drugs Róisín had to take for most of her life; the national health services treated without charge. The nursing care, warm and skilful, especially from the ward sister — the

Preface

key person where families are concerned — sustained us for many years.

But all this sophisticated treatment was aimed at cure; it seemed that by contrast there was no system, no programme yet devised to care for children who could not be cured. It was a great shock to find that no one appeared to be prepared for, or quite knew how to achieve, the task of comforting our dying child. She had had leukaemia for ten years, a disease which in its terminal phases can be painless, but can also cause excruciating bone pain.

The hospital eventually brought Róisín's pain under control by ensuring that she got regular morphine in the dosage and frequency she needed. Thanks to Our Lady's Hospice home-care team we were able to bring her home. The hospice team anticipated problems and were available day and night, making possible the peace that we all needed for those last ten days or so. We are deeply grateful to them, and to the hospital teams which gave us extra years with Róisín.

But the gap in care into which we had fallen so shocked me that I felt attention should be drawn to this area of need.

People ask if it is through indifference that children's suffering in terminal illness is left unassuaged. I believe that failure to develop proper systems of care stems more from lack of awareness than from callousness. I hope that this book will contribute to a greater understanding of the needs of dying children and their families, and that out of that greater understanding will come action to relieve their suffering.

Acknowledgements

This book is based on my dissertation for the degree of Master of Science (Community Health) of Trinity College, Dublin.

I would like to thank my supervisor, Professor James McCormick, for his support and encouragement; Dr Fin Breatnach and Ms Gail O'Sullivan of Our Lady's Hospital for Sick Children, Crumlin, for their assistance in contacting families to take part in the study and for their interest in the project, and the other doctors and nurses who also helped, but who for reasons of confidentiality cannot be named.

I would particularly like to thank all the parents who so generously took part in the study.

I am very grateful to Colm Hanley of Printset and Design and Criterion Press who very generously sponsored the production costs of this book, thereby making publication possible.

Finally I would like to thank my husband Tony, without whom neither the research nor the book would ever have been completed.

CHAPTER 1

Cancer and children

'No one ever expects their child to get cancer....'

Few children get cancer. Less than three per cent of all cases of cancer occur in children under fourteen years of age. Yet, in the richer countries of the world, cancer is the second most common cause of death in childhood (accidents are the leading cause).[1] Three hundred or so children aged one to fourteen die every year in Ireland; of these, about forty die of some form of cancer.[2] In the UK there are about five hundred such deaths every year out of a total of 2500.[3]

About one in seven hundred children develop cancer.[4] World-wide, leukaemia is the most common form, followed by malignancies of the central nervous system.[5] In Ireland, the average annual incidence rate of the most common type of leukaemia, acute lymphoblastic, (which is what our daughter had) is thirty-one per million children. This rate is similar to that of other Western populations.[6]

Little is known about trends in the incidence of childhood cancer but the Manchester Children's Tumour Registry, which covers a population of about one million children, recorded a significant increase in the incidence of acute lymphoblastic leukaemia between 1954 and 1977; similar increases were recorded in Sweden and Finland.[7] Significantly more boys than girls develop cancer (there is a thirty per cent excess incidence of acute lymphoblastic leukaemia in boys, fifty per cent excess incidence over all), and children with Down's Syndrome have an excess risk of developing leukaemia.[8]

We do not know exactly what causes cancer in children, although it is clear that both genetic and environmental factors contribute to certain malignancies. We do know, however, that X-raying pregnant women, and exposing fathers to irradiation before their children are conceived, increase the chances of their children developing leukaemia.[9]

A generation ago, childhood cancer was almost invariably fatal. Today, treatment has advanced so much that more than half of all children with cancer, who receive the most up to date treatment, survive to adulthood. Some forms of childhood cancer, including acute lymphoblastic leukaemia, are regarded as 'curable'; others are classified as chronic life-threatening diseases. Thus more children are now living longer with cancer.[10]

Yet even with the most advanced treatment, at least a third of all children with cancer die in childhood. Some die suddenly and unexpectedly from complications of disease or treatment; some deaths are unexpected because of failure to recognise that treatment aimed at cure is no longer appropriate and the child is in fact terminally ill; but the majority of children with fatal cancer die after a period during which death was expected and for which terminal care could therefore be planned.[11] It is with such children that this book is concerned.

A great deal is now known and published about the needs of people who are dying and of their families. The hospice movement has highlighted the importance of symptom control combined with social, psychological, spiritual and emotional support. A number of models of excellent terminal care have been documented.[12] Children who are dying also need symptom control, and they and their families need a great deal of support.[13]

However, perhaps partly because the numbers involved are so small, and also because people find it so hard to face the fact of a child dying, the plight of terminally ill children and their families received little attention until quite recently. Neither paediatricians nor the hospice movement gave much attention to children's needs for symptom control and good terminal care. This has resulted in a dearth of specialist knowledge on how best to relieve difficult symptoms and how to support the family as a whole.[14]

Adolescents are perhaps the most vulnerable, and most neglected, of all the age groups.[15] Case studies, clinicians'

Cancer and children

reports and anecdotal evidence all suggest that dying children and their families receive less support and skilled symptom control than is needed to alleviate their distress.[16] The aim of good terminal care, according to a recent UK working party, is to help families achieve the best possible quality of life for their dying children.[17] But we know very little about how well this goal is achieved in practice.

This book presents the experiences of twenty families, related from the parents' points of view and largely through their words (the interviews were tape-recorded). Through them we catch a glimpse of what it means to care for a dying child, and the anguish endured by children and parents alike when proper care is not made available.

The children concerned were aged from two to fifteen when they died, and all except one had cancer; the exception was a child who suffered from a rare syndrome akin to cystic fibrosis. Those interviewed included a quarter of the families of children who had died of cancer in Ireland during the study period. They came from a variety of places and backgrounds, and included farmers, professionals and factory workers. (The Appendix gives a full account of the method and sample used in the study.)

I interviewed mothers and fathers together in the family home. These were not formal interviews with lists of predetermined questions; rather, I invited the parents to tell me about their child's illness, beginning with the diagnosis of life-threatening disease: what happened, what support they had received from health and social services, from family, neighbours, clergy, and the wider community; what had helped, what had made the situation even worse, and what could have been done better.

Of course they talked about much more than practical matters. Heavy with sorrow, they were preoccupied with memories of their dead children and were eager to share them. They offered many insights into their own and their children's reactions to their trial, their struggle to come to terms with what was happening, and the ways in which their outlook on life had been changed by their child's illness and death.

They remembered with pride their lost children, painting vivid pictures of the sons and daughters who were gone: the young boy with the loud, confident voice who enjoyed football and climbing trees but always had his shirt neatly tucked in; the imperious little girl who loved her doctor and used to scold her mother for delaying the departure to hospital; the gentle twelve-year-old whose doctor called her 'my smiling girl', who throughout her illness 'passed no scene at all, even when she lost her leg'; the teenage boy who, when he could no longer see well enough to play darts, pretended he had lost interest, and later confided to his mother that he thought he could live without his sight.

They showed me photographs: of the bright-eyed girls and boys, sometimes dressed up for Communion or Confirmation, sometimes in their jeans and T-shirts, riding bicycles, arms around their brothers and sisters. Photographs of the child who had died, as well as of the other children in the family, were displayed in all the homes I visited.

The parents knew that I too had lost a child, and this shared experience meant that we met on common ground. Many of them told me that it was because of this that they agreed to take part in the study.

All of the interviews were intense, and extremely emotional at times. As might be expected, tears were shed on many occasions, by fathers as well as mothers. Yet the situation was controlled and the emotion contained without difficulty in all cases, with an implicit understanding between us all that such control was necessary and desirable.

Some of the families had received all the support they felt they needed, but the majority recalled episodes when their child's pain went out of control or they themselves felt alone and abandoned. A few families described failures in care which had resulted in great suffering.

In most of the interviews, parents spoke with little or no prompting and eagerly seized the opportunity to talk at length about their children, the fatal illnesses, the grief which dominated their thoughts and feelings. At times couples spoke in a rush, both together, supplementing each other's memories. The narrative slowed and stopped for a time when they recalled the child's death, and this was the point in the interview when tears were most often shed.

Mothers were the main speakers in nine of the interviews, parents shared the narrative more or less equally in another nine, and the father was the main speaker in two interviews.

Three fathers had expressed some reluctance to participate before the interview took place; one father doubted his ability to take part, another thought that since his wife had done most of the nursing of their sick child he would have little to contribute. In the event, both of these fathers, like all of the other participants, made significant contributions to the study.

On occasion, the more silent partner was clearly longing to intervene or to add something while the narrative rushed on, the parent who was speaking intent on making a point or clarifying a memory. Parents were generally in agreement about what had actually happened, although there was confusion occasionally about sequences of events. Husbands' and wives' interpretations or judgements differed from time to time — a mother, for example, softening her husband's criticisms of what he saw as the failures of the medical system.

The style of narrative varied from couple to couple. Some told their story in a low-key way, others used highly charged language to convey their reactions and feelings. For example, the words 'horror' and 'fear' recurred throughout three interviews whereas another couple used no emotive words at all in their intensely moving account of their child's short life.

Many of the parents looked exhausted and strained; their sorrow and struggle to come to terms with their loss was often expressed in such remarks as 'You'd wonder why'.

This book presents the families' experiences in roughly chronological order, beginning, in Chapter 2, with the diagnosis of life-threatening disease.

CHAPTER 2

The bombshell

'That's how it all started...the long, hard road, as you know.'

The diagnosis of cancer in their children was a watershed in the lives of all the parents I interviewed. It marked the end of normal family living and the beginning of another life, filled with grief, uncertainty, disruption of normal activities, and fear of the future. As the father of a little boy who died from a neuroblastoma said: 'It was a sentence that was given to us the day he was diagnosed, and we're still carrying it.'

Although for some parents the diagnosis came out of the blue, and a number said that they had not previously known that children could get cancer, most had begun to suspect that something was seriously wrong; and a few, observing all the signs and symptoms, had already realised what was later confirmed.

The symptoms leading up to the diagnosis included fever, lassitude, pallor, pain in the abdomen, back or legs, swellings on limbs, abdomen or head, headaches, vomiting, dark patches under the eyes, and bruising. Some of the children appeared to be quite well apart from the swellings or episodes of pain; others were clearly unwell, while four were obviously very ill. An adolescent boy remarked after he was admitted to hospital for a brain scan: 'I'm so relieved to be in hospital because I hope they'll do something for this headache.' 'It was then', said his mother, 'we realised how bad he was.'

Another adolescent boy, with a lump in his leg, went gaily off to hospital casualty with his brother. His mother remembered telling them to wait until the evening to see the doctor, but they wouldn't listen. 'They were laughing, they wanted a morning off school.' Osteosarcoma, a form of bone cancer, was diagnosed a few days later.

All of the other children were seen first by their family

The bombshell

doctors, who in most cases referred them to hospital within hours or days. Delays occurred in three cases due to GPs misdiagnosing or failing to take symptoms seriously. These delays amounted to a fortnight in two cases and some months in another.

Once they were referred to specialists, most of the children were diagnosed within a few days. However, delays were experienced by six families.

One couple who strongly suspected that their nine-year-old son had leukaemia, waited in anguish for over a week for the results of tests.

A twelve-year-old girl with a swelling in her leg was referred for X-ray, but there was a two-week delay during which time her tumour, which was hot and had to be cooled with ice, was growing.

A toddler of eighteen months with a prominent lump on her forehead, who was 'pale as a ghost, and very sore to touch', was X-rayed, but when no fracture was found the specialist in a local hospital dismissed the parents. The GP intervened, scolding the consultant over the phone in the parents' hearing — 'She was very annoyed, she was fantastic' — and the little girl was referred to a specialist unit where it was found that she had a tumour which was very far advanced — a stage four neuroblastoma.

A three-year-old boy with pains in his legs was referred after a week's delay to a children's hospital where he and his mother spent another two weeks before cancer was diagnosed. During that fortnight he endured considerable pain and lost a stone in weight. He was given pain-killers. 'He was on Ponstan for pain before he came in; that was stopped and he was put on a teaspoon of Dozol at bedtime. He never slept for a fortnight. He was in pain all the time.' The pains in his legs turned out to be due to advanced cancer.

A child with chronic pain at the base of her spine from early childhood, underwent numerous investigations over the years. Her parents were very hurt by the scepticism of doctors who labelled them over-anxious, telling them in so many words that most of their daughter's pain was 'the result of what we were telling her and that we were playing up to her'. Treatment, including surgery, brought no relief, and the parents were told that their daughter would have to put up with the pain. 'We comforted her as best we could when she got the pain...far too many nights we'd find her sitting up in bed complaining about the pain in her back.' After other symptoms appeared, medical scepticism receded and the parents heard the consultant comment: 'Certainly we have something more here than parental anxiety.' It transpired that the child had a malignant tumour, probably since birth.

A five-year-old was initially thought to have leukaemia. Eventually her condition, a syndrome of immune deficiencies, similar in some respects to cystic fibrosis, was diagnosed and her mother was told: 'It's like leukaemia, only worse.'

The diagnosis
Even when expected, the actual diagnosis of life-threatening disease came as a frightful shock. In interview after interview, parents used the words 'bombshell' and 'nightmare' to evoke their reactions.

One father said he nearly fainted when told his child had cancer. Two other fathers described their physical reactions: 'It was horror. I thought I was going to lose control of my bowels there and then.' 'I was losing control totally, my whole body was shaking, I thought my head was going to fall off my shoulders.'

A mother described how the doctor giving the diagnosis recognised her shock and insisted she have a cup of tea before driving home. 'She must have seen something in my face — she followed me out to the car park to make sure I was all right to drive.'

A number of parents said that the initial diagnosis was the greatest shock in all of the illness: 'I think that was the worst shock of all, really, trying to come to terms with it.' 'The initial diagnosis was a nightmare, it was the worst part of it.' A father said, 'It was a full week before I could even think', and he

The bombshell

added that although later events were also devastating, he never again went into the same trance-like state of shock.

Some parents could not take in the diagnosis and remembered their disbelief: 'It was unbelievable when they told us.' 'To tell you the truth I didn't believe them at the time.' 'I didn't really believe it as it was happening.' A mother commented: 'It takes weeks for it to sink in, what's actually happening.'

Such reactions and comments are strikingly similar to those reported in other studies of parents' reactions to the diagnosis of life-threatening disease in their child: feelings of disbelief, shock and grief; the blow to their sense of security; feelings of helplessness and guilt.[1] One mother wrote of her 'feeling of total inadequacy, of total failure. Because perhaps deep down, particularly for a mother, you feel your first job is that your child should survive....'[2]

Anger too, is often felt, and is sometimes directed at those giving the bad news. Only two of the couples I interviewed mentioned anger in connection with the diagnosis. One mother said she actually struck the paediatrician when he told her that her daughter was terminally ill. She had already built up an excellent relationship with this doctor over the months following the initial diagnosis; he was very supportive to the whole family throughout the child's illness.

Another couple remembered being asked by the informing medical team if they felt angry that their son had cancer. This couple, who were perhaps the most serene of all the parents I interviewed, were much perplexed by the question. 'We were surprised by that. We discussed it afterwards and we felt honestly we never felt angry.'

Many of the mothers mentioned how much they had cried in the days following the diagnosis. 'The first day [in hospital] I couldn't stop crying.' A father, when told his only son had leukaemia, wept unrestrainedly in the hospital foyer. Another father was sent home from work because he cried so much. As one father remarked: 'There's no handy way of getting that type of news.'

Nonetheless, the manner in which the diagnosis was given was vividly described by a number of parents. They expressed gratitude when the medical team had conveyed the information clearly and honestly, had appeared to care about the child and had supported them in their distress; they felt hurt when the diagnosis had been thrust on them in public places, without regard for the emotional effects of such news. On several occasions doctors later apologised to parents for the insensitivity of their colleagues.

One couple were standing in the doorway of the ward in which their sick child lay when they were told that he had a tumour and it might not be possible to remove it: 'You couldn't see gravity to be told a thing like that so fast. If we were brought into an office or something, but we weren't even sitting down.' The father went to get a chair for his wife who was pregnant, but he nearly fainted himself.

Another father was standing in a hospital corridor when the surgeon, accompanied by his team, told him his daughter had an inoperable tumour. 'I thought their eyes were pokers and that they were boring holes in me…. I was conscious of these eyes taking me apart and I just walked away.'

Many parents spoke with appreciation of the manner in which one particular consultant, who cared for the majority of the children in this study, gave them the diagnosis and explained the situation. Typical comments from parents of all backgrounds were: 'He brought me into a room, and the one thing I remember is he sat there, he showed no signs of wanting to go, or being busy, or that he was expecting someone else. He was totally honest that day, he was fantastic.' 'It was extraordinarily sensitively done. We spent one and a half hours with him, but we felt that if we had needed five hours he would have given it.' 'He broke it in such a way you could accept it. He'd say so much to you and then he'd wait, and when you'd absorbed it he'd come again.'

Such approving comments echo those of seventy families interviewed in 1989 in the UK about the diagnosis of life-threatening disease in their children. The researchers found that parents vividly remembered, even years later, how they were informed, and how doctors responded to their distress. They greatly appreciated privacy, doctors' sympathetic, unhurried manner, honesty, and the opportunity to ask questions and have information repeated and clarified. Furthermore, 'The doctor's ability to accept and understand the parents' grief was important in establishing trust and shaping the future relationship.'[3]

Immediate reactions
Shocked and grief-stricken, some of the parents could not immediately face their children, whose loss appeared suddenly so imminent. A mother said: 'I just burst into tears in the corridor, and I thought "I can never go back in the ward, I can't look at him, I have to get out of here", and that's exactly what I did.... I sent my sister into the room to get my bag and then we went to the shopping centre and I bought him a pair of pyjamas. I didn't know what I was doing, but I just could not go straight back into the room with him.'

The mother of a little girl with neuroblastoma said that it would have been helpful in the hard days after the diagnosis to have met another parent who had been through it. 'Someone to say "Look, it's all right, you're not going to die under all this shock", not to discuss her chances of living or dying but to tell us "You'll be all right, you'll get there, you're not going to feel this bad all the time", to give us the strength, then we could have been a bit stronger for her.'

Some consultants appeared to be sensitive to these reactions and gave parents a breathing space before discussing prognoses or decisions about aggressive treatment. 'We were in such a state, and he said "Would you like to go home for the weekend?"'

A father who had been abroad when his son was diagnosed commented approvingly: 'The doctor didn't come near me for two days. He didn't want to throw everything at me.'

In other cases, no doubt because life-saving treatment had to begin immediately, everything seemed to happen at once.

'That's how it all started', said the mother of a child who died of leukaemia, 'into isolation and all the rest, the long hard road, as you know.'

CHAPTER 3

An uncertain future

'In the beginning you need lots of hope....'

When a child is diagnosed with cancer 'the best the physician can offer is hope expressed as a probability, based on statistics for cure or death'.[1] The future includes death for some children, although which children cannot always be predicted; for this reason, some clinicians consider that terminal care begins at diagnosis.[2]

Various possible sequences of treatment and care following diagnosis of cancer, and depending on prognosis, are shown in Figure 1 on page 24. When the form of disease is thought to be curable, treatment is aimed primarily at cure. When curative treatment is not effective, the aim may change, gradually or quickly, from cure to life extension or palliation.

Some children whose form of disease is almost inevitably fatal, may have their lives extended by treatments which are known to have a temporary effect. For other children, the main aim of treatment, from initial diagnosis, is to minimise the child's discomfort and pain, not to cure or prolong life.

The sequences as set out in Figure 1 should be seen as continuous, from cure to life-extension, to palliation, to symptom control, rather than as sharply distinguished stages. Treatment decisions are not always clear-cut and many therapies offer curative, life-extending and palliative possibilities.[3] It is the primary intent of the treatment which is signalled here, not the nature of the treatment itself.

Treatment for cancer usually involves chemotherapy and radiotherapy, and often mutilating surgery as well. The drugs are highly toxic and can cause most unpleasant reactions, such as nausea, hair loss, mood change, and impaired intelligence. Steroids can lead to obesity. Both curative and life-extending treatments are often aptly named 'aggressive' and sometimes

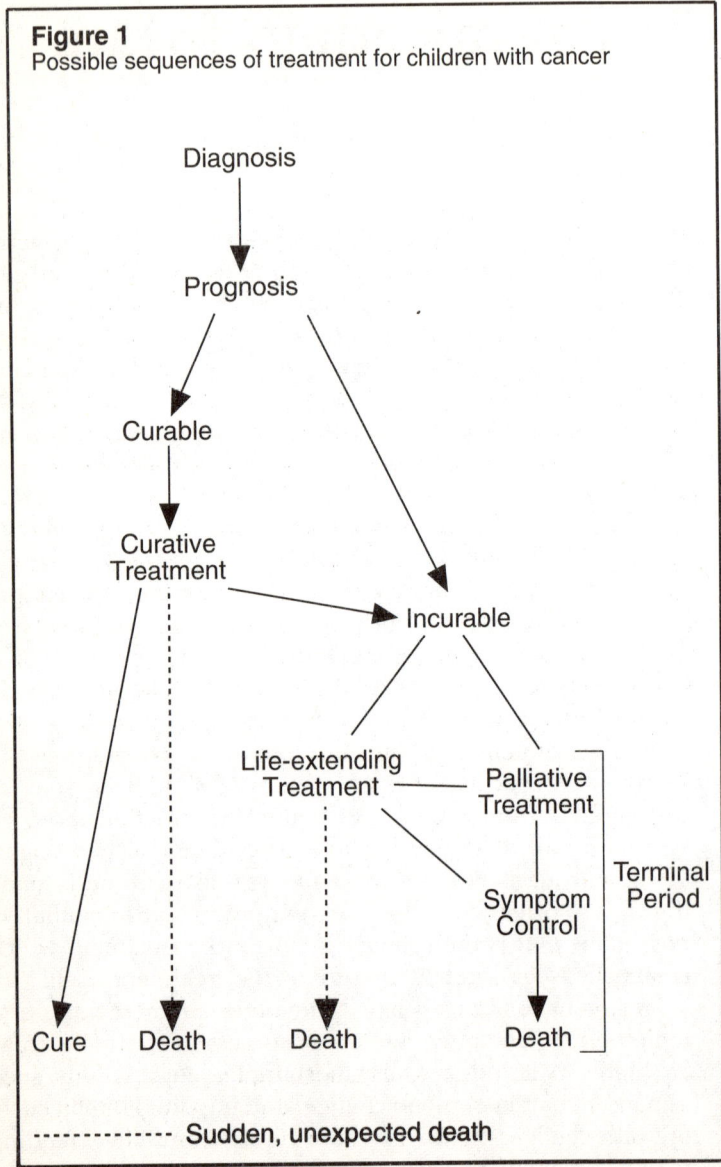

Figure 1
Possible sequences of treatment for children with cancer

An uncertain future

result in sudden death due, for example, to catastrophic infection or toxic reaction.

The procedures for giving the treatment or for diagnosis are often painful and usually involve needles; they range from simple blood tests to bone-marrow aspirations and lumbar punctures. One study found that the major cause of pain in children with cancer related to the treatment rather than the disease.[4]

Parents are often powerless to prevent their children's suffering when undergoing diagnostic or treatment procedures, although they may be able to reduce it. It is very hard to have to watch helplessly while one's child suffers; this affront to parental instincts can leave mothers and fathers with an abiding sense of failure and guilt.[5]

Yet unpleasant and painful though treatment may be, the alternative can be worse: untreated disease may result not only in death but also in symptoms far worse than those produced when disease is even partially controlled.[6]

Many children are cured of cancer, and for a time at least some of the parents in this study had reasonable hopes that their children might survive. In a number of cases, disease was controlled (but not removed) for many months. For example, one child responded well to treatment for leukaemia and remained in remission for several years, only to develop a fatal brain tumour.

Some parents grasped at whatever hope was offered and interpreted estimates of their child's chances in the most optimistic light: 'The doctor said he had a fifty/fifty chance, but as far as we were concerned it was our fifty per cent.' 'He didn't say "Take her home, she's going to die", he said she had a twenty-five per cent chance."' 'He said she had a fifty per cent chance, which we thought was absolutely marvellous.'

Such optimism helped to sustain parents' morale during long periods of uncertainty. It was especially necessary when children had to undergo prolonged, unpleasant treatment. As one mother said: 'In the beginning you need lots of hope, you need to tell yourselves "Maybe we'll be one of the lucky ones".

We had a lot of hope, too, in the beginning.' This perception was shared by the father of another child: 'We needed hope at the time, even the tiniest hope.'

Other parents recalled that from the outset their children's prospects were very poor, although active treatment with curative or life-extending intent was given in some cases. 'The scenario was very bleak.' 'The doctor didn't think there was much of a chance for him at all.' 'We were never, ever, told [there was a chance of] cure.'

Two of the children had a form of incurable cancer and their treatment was aimed only at palliation; they entered the terminal period at diagnosis. All of the other children underwent 'active' treatment aimed at cure or life-extension, including chemotherapy, surgery (mainly to remove tumours and including limb amputations) and/or radiation, or a combination of therapies. Twelve of the children suffered episodes of acute and sometimes critical illness during the period of active treatment.

Thirteen children died within eighteen months of diagnosis, while six survived for several years after diagnosis. The child with the immune problem lived for a number of years after diagnosis. The shortest period of survival for the children with cancer was five months and the longest was three and a half years.

Figure 2 on page 27 shows the number of months which elapsed between initial diagnosis and terminal diagnosis, and between terminal diagnosis and death for each of the children concerned. While some of the children were quite well when they entered the terminal period, others were already dying at this point.[7]

Treatment centres
To have the best chance of cure, children should come under the care of specialist centres which have a caseload of at least fifty new cases of childhood cancer every year. 'There is no place for the single-handed, occasional paediatric oncologist in present-day practice.'[8] Only in such centres can the

An uncertain future

Figure 2
Number of months elapsing between initial diagnosis and terminal diagnosis, and between terminal diagnosis and death of the children with cancer. The period of active treatment includes both curative and life-extending treatment.

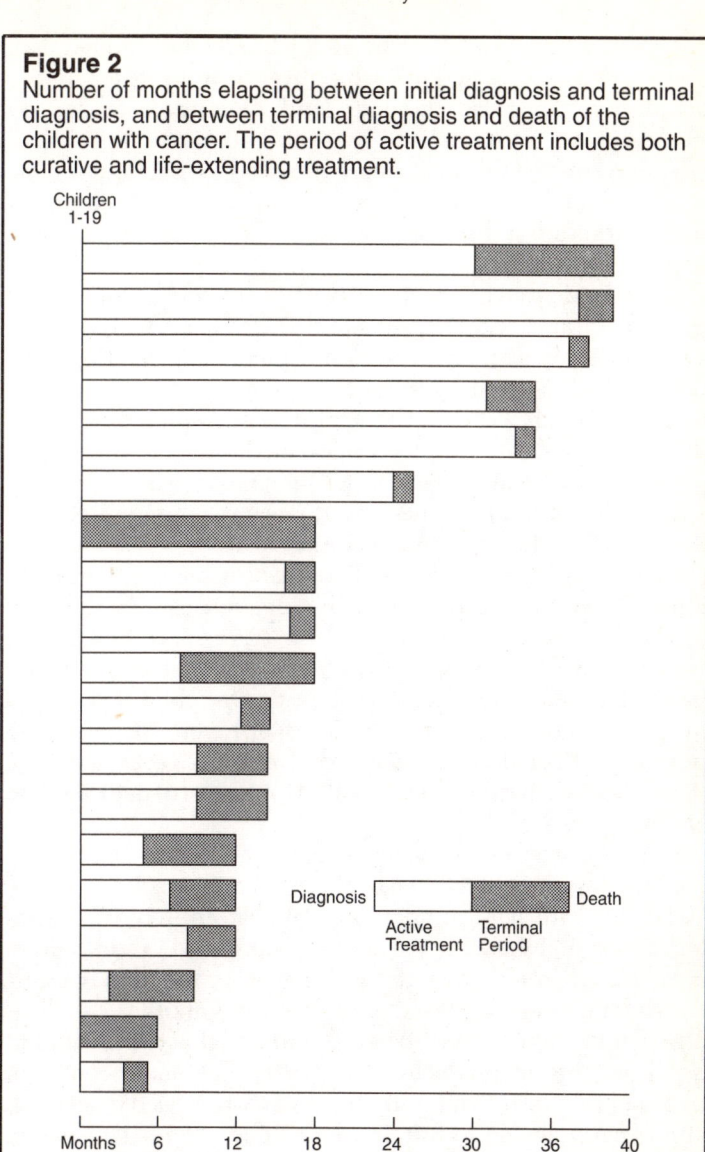

necessary expertise in planning and treatment be acquired. Not only do children treated in such centres have a greater chance of survival, but also the pain and discomfort caused by treatment can be minimised by skilful administration.[9]

Systems of shared care, where the child's treatment regime is devised in a specialist centre but maintenance therapy and routine tests are carried out in a hospital nearer home, are often appropriate.[10]

Childhood cancer centres usually develop social and psychological support systems for the families who must live, sometimes for many years, with a potentially fatal disease. During the long course of treatment, families usually come to trust and rely heavily on the staff in the hospital unit where their child is treated, not only for medical care but also for practical and emotional support. Often GPs are little involved with the child, and parents find themselves going directly to the hospital with any problems that arise.[11]

Of the nineteen children with cancer whose parents I interviewed, twelve received most of their care in the only centre in Ireland which meets the criteria set out above. Another child's care was shared between that centre and a paediatrician in a hospital nearer home. One child was treated by a succession of consultants for over a year, before being referred to the children's cancer centre some weeks before he died. Three children were treated in a ward dedicated to children's cancer.

Two adolescent boys were treated in adult wards, and one of them appears not to have been seen by an oncologist at any stage, his care being undertaken almost entirely by neurologists. The child with the disease similar to cystic fibrosis received treatment over a number of years from various consultants, her care passing from one to another.

Seven of the children received additional active treatment as in-patients in hospitals other than their main centre of treatment. Four had amputations in an orthopaedic hospital, and three travelled to Britain for full-body irradiation before having bone-marrow transplants in the children's cancer centre.

An uncertain future

Other hospitals were also involved from time to time in the course of many of the children's illnesses: for emergency admissions to control pain, for specialist services such as scans and radiation, not available in the main centre of treatment, and for initial diagnoses before referral to specialist centres. Some children received treatment in three or more different hospitals, whereas others had treatment in only one or two hospitals. A total of fifteen hospitals in Ireland and three in Britain were mentioned as having been involved at some stage in the children's illnesses.

All of the children spent periods of varying lengths as in-patients in hospital and most had repeated stays in hospital. One child stayed in hospital for nearly a year after a ten-hour operation to remove a tumour. Eight other children spent more than two months in hospital, without returning home.

Thus hospitals, doctors and nurses played a very important part in all of the families' lives, during the period immediately following diagnosis and, for some families, throughout the illness. Five children died in the hospitals where they received their main treatment.

One of the issues that arose again and again in the course of my interviews with the parents was their need for good, clear communication with the medical teams caring for their children. This is the subject of the next chapter.

CHAPTER 4

Getting information, making decisions

'If you have knowledge you can deal with it, once you know the worst ... knowing what's ahead of you, no matter how dreadful.'

Throughout their child's illness, but especially in the weeks immediately following diagnosis of life-threatening disease, the parents needed a mass of detailed information: about the disease, its type and severity, how it might progress and with what consequences, the implications of various courses of action, the treatment available and the prospects of cure, the risks and side-effects of aggressive therapy, what to expect, what to look out for, where to go for help, what their entitlements were.

Knowledge and sympathetic support were needed to help them to come to terms with the fact that their child had a life-threatening disease, to care for their child in hospital and at home, to care for their other children and each other, to organise their families' lives in the short term, and to prepare for a most uncertain future. As one mother I interviewed remarked: 'If you have knowledge you can deal with it ... knowing what's ahead of you, no matter how dreadful. You have unnecessary fears if you're left in a twilight.'

Such needs are now increasingly recognised by professionals, and children's cancer units often include specialist social workers and staff trained in communicating with, and supporting, families.

Asked what kind of help they would like, parents tend to look for 'someone who has specific knowledge of the child's illness and treatment, an understanding of the stresses and emotional difficulties, plus a knowledge of counselling skills'.[1]

Getting information, making decisions

Communication

The parents I interviewed were largely dependent on their medical advisers and, to a lesser degree, on other professional people such as nurses and social workers, to keep them informed and to help them understand and come to terms with their predicament.

Most parents said that doctors had 'done their best' to explain the situation and keep them informed, with comments ranging from the lukewarm 'He did try to explain to the best of his ability', to the positively enthusiastic 'I couldn't speak too highly of his ability to communicate his skilled knowledge and to treat us, not as equals, but as partners.'

However, one couple experienced great difficulty getting any information at all. 'We didn't know what was happening. For information, you see, we were depending on the doctor.' They had to wait two weeks for a discussion about the outcome of their son's operation to remove a brain tumour, and they spent many hours waiting around on the off-chance of seeing a doctor. 'He wouldn't actually come to see us — if we were lucky enough and he was around, we'd see him. That sort of thing happened all the time.' The strain of 'trying to grab information from everybody', being fobbed off — 'They used to tell us it was complicated and that was it' — and waiting with their sick child in queues of up to one hundred people to meet a doctor who might then leave before seeing them, led this family to opt for private medical care and to pay for treatment that they could ill afford. 'Once you pay, that's it, that's different.' But later, when their son developed secondaries, the parents found themselves again waiting around in corridors, trying to get information, and dealing with various consultants.

Two other couples, both from professional backgrounds, complained about the content and manner of doctors' communication. 'These doctors and surgeons talk to you as if you were one of them and you know exactly what they're saying.... I cannot say the doctor did not tell us the facts, he did, but he told us in a calm, cool, collected way as if he was lecturing to a group of medical students, not to two people who were in deep shock.' The pattern continued, with other consultants discussing the medical side and no more. 'There was no communication really. We were told very little; everything was done but so little was explained.' Discussions were often held without privacy: 'This is something that featured again and again — consultations in corridors with the world passing by.'

The second couple remarked of their child's consultant: 'He was always busy; he would never sit down and just talk to us, and when he did [talk] he had swallowed a dictionary and we were always trying to sort out the Latin terms in our heads — we weren't taking in what he was saying.'

A mother commented on the need to be properly informed so as to be able to meet doctors on the same level: 'The great thing is not to allow yourself to be intimidated by all the jargon. Terms — what are they? They're words, they may sound very difficult but once you understand them and what they stand for, they're a reference point. You have to know and be clued in and then they [the doctors] respect that.'

Doctors, even when good at communicating, were generally perceived as busy. 'We were always conscious that his time was limited.' 'Doctors are under pressure and you don't want to take too much of their time.'

Some of the parents tried to supplement consultations by reading and questioning third parties: 'We read every possible thing about it and asked every possible kind of question.' A mother criticised the quality of material available: 'I just couldn't get my hands on readable stuff; the [social workers] did give me some stuff but I found it was all American and they had different approaches and different drugs; what I wanted was a book which would explain in layman's language so that we could be very well versed when talking to doctors, but I just never came across that.'

One couple regretted that it was only late in their son's illness that they were given literature to explain his disease: 'If we had had the literature it would all have made sense.'

The use of terms such as 'serious', or jargon such as

Getting information, making decisions

'malignant', without explanation, misled parents on occasion. Thus a mother who had been informed that her child had a malignant tumour and that it was 'serious' said: 'I was taken aback all right' but 'I didn't understand what malignant meant.... It wasn't explained that much and I suppose it didn't mean anything to me, the lump [tumour] was there and they were going to take it out and that was it.'

The parents of two boys with brain tumours were unaware until the late stages in their sons' illnesses that cancer was the major problem.

Particularly misleading was the description of surgery as 'successful'. A number of parents were led to believe that because surgery was successful, in the sense that tumours were removed with minimum damage to function (although in some cases this involved amputating limbs), that the problem was now solved. Parents of two girls who had surgery to remove tumours thought for a while that they were cured: 'I thought after the operation she was cured, she made such a good recovery.' 'When she survived the operation we thought she was cured.'

The parents of two children who had amputations also thought the surgery had solved the problem: 'I didn't think she'd die. I thought she'd make it. You see, in the beginning I didn't know about secondaries, about these cancer cells and how they flow through the blood. I was innocent to all that. I thought once she'd have her amputation, even though her leg would be gone, we'd have her at least.'

Although most of the parents found that doctors at least tried to keep them informed, successful communication was not always achieved. For example, when a father said, 'He explained everything. If you had a problem, and made an arrangement, he was there', his wife added, 'Even if you didn't understand....' A number of parents recalled how little they understood and said they often felt baffled and ill-informed: 'We were really lost, we knew nothing, we didn't know what to expect.' 'I never understood anything. I didn't know what tumour it was, but they could have cut it down and told me in little words, but I didn't understand.' 'He'd go into a lot of details that you might never understand but he'd still let you know. The trouble was, I found that if it was something serious it had to be explained two or three times, maybe today and tomorrow again.' 'The doctor used to say, "Ask me anything you want to know"; sure, we didn't know what we wanted to know, we didn't know what was happening to our boy. "Go home tonight," the doctor said, "and sit down and write down your questions." We never knew what questions to ask.' 'When you start out with a sick child you're terrified to ask any questions. When you see all those people the questions disappear.' 'You are so shocked in the beginning that you don't take it in at all. The doctor was great and he did explain, but you come home and you wonder.'

Parents from all backgrounds expressed the need for counselling to supplement medical consultations: 'I think what really would have helped us was counselling, someone really making us listen, not to give up hope; but to actually understand what is happening, and not during the two weeks after diagnosis, because it's such a shock.' 'There's too much to cope with and there's definitely too little counselling.'

Counselling was seen as the giving of information in an unhurried atmosphere, sympathetically, in language that could be understood, which helped parents to 'take it on board'. 'When your child has cancer someone really should sit down with you and tell you what it is and all about it, in your own words, not in the book words they use, so that you'll understand. Because they speak words that confuse you altogether, even confuse the doctors, I think.' 'No one ever spoke to us or came to us; [a nurse] was very good and very nice but she didn't have much time, there was never anyone really to go and talk to.'

A mother said: 'The social worker and all were very good to us but we'd rather have someone that we could sit down with and could explain the problems to, like another parent that went through it, that sort of knows what you're going through.' She wanted someone on hand in the ward to explain

Getting information, making decisions

what was happening to her child, the progress of the treatment and her condition. 'Somebody to talk to you and explain the ups and downs of chemotherapy, ''This is doing her good and this is doing her bad and she'll have up days and down days.'' But nobody really sat down, you were just all worried and feeling alone and had nobody to talk to, except for the mothers. You were kind of looking for a bit of support, but [the other mothers were] going through the exact same thing as you're going through. Another mother couldn't give you support when her own child was being sick.'

A few parents mentioned their worry when the child first came home after diagnosis. One father explained: 'It's really when you come home first that you need someone to go through it with you. You're in such a daze [in the hospital] that you don't take it in. When you sit down in your own surroundings you need someone to call then and explain to you how sick he will get. We were told he would be sick, but how sick is sick? I think at that stage there's not enough counselling, you'd want someone to call to the house and tell you exactly. He'd get so low so quickly. We didn't understand that, we didn't have a clue, that's being honest about it. You're left with this very sick child.'

One mother said that the only person to counsel her and her husband, 'the only one who ever spoke to us', was a nurse/counsellor in an orthopaedic hospital, who helped parents and children to come to terms with the loss of limbs. 'They were building us up to tell us he'd have an amputation.... I nearly went mad, I went crazy, the idea of him losing his leg. She was telling us that he would be able to get an artificial leg and lead a normal life. We just thought his leg was going to come off.' The positive approach left these parents with the impression that their son would definitely be cured. They were told the operation to remove his leg had been 'one hundred per cent successful'. 'We just thought he was going to lose his leg.'

A mother commented on the optimistic attitude of another unit: 'They always tried to put the good side out, it would annoy you but at the same time you could understand their position. They're trying to keep you going. I presume they're saying to themselves "If they throw in the towel they'll be no good to the child".' Her husband added: 'There seems to be a thing with doctors that they will only give you as much information as they think you can take, or that you will ask for, and if you don't ask they won't tell you anything. They tell you so much but then they expect you to deduce from that, and if you're not [well-informed] you can be left in an ignorant state.'

Paternalism was evident in one incident. When this father read an article from a medical journal in a children's ward he discovered from it that his son had a very poor prognosis. 'I remember sitting at the nurse's station one night — they screen everything — but I just noticed this report, a photocopy on relapses in leukaemia from the New England School of Medicine, and although I didn't understand everything I got the gist of it.' Faced with his clear understanding, doctors conceded that the child was indeed 'on time'. This was a crucial piece of information which determined how the family approached the rest of the boy's life. Knowing his death was now inevitable they decided that quality not length of life was paramount and were able to put their energies not into cure but into making his and their last months as enjoyable as possible. The day after the discussion, however, the article and 'all the paediatric textbooks disappeared out of the ward'.

Honesty, openness and availability of medical staff were highly valued by parents of all backgrounds: 'The best of them was they never left you in any doubt as to what was going on, no matter how hard a thing was they told you.' 'The doctor in session was very straight and open and would tell you everything you wanted to know.' 'At that first meeting he didn't try to camouflage anything, he laid everything out in the gentlest possible way.' A teenage boy remarked to a family friend that he trusted one doctor more than another 'because he told me straight out that [a treatment] might work and it might not and if it doesn't I'll die. I prefer him to be honest.'

Parents did not want fudging or prevarication: 'I didn't want anyone beating around the bush, saying "There are no absolutes". I said "I want it, I want the truth".' 'We always demanded candour, [we did not want] hedging and not giving the full truth.' One mother said frankly: 'I only wanted to know my son was getting better.'

A few parents noted how their needs changed over time: 'There are stages when you don't want the gory details, can't cope with them, but you get over those stages and your need to know is greater than your queasiness.' 'I didn't go into that meeting [to discuss the child's prognosis], I didn't want to know; I am a different person now.'

Some parents mentioned in the course of the interview that they and/or doctors had explained to their children that their condition was serious but that it was hoped and expected that the treatment would make them better. The parents of three of the older children said that they 'wanted to know what was going on'. 'We always had to explain the ins and outs of everything.' A fourteen-year-old girl became very annoyed when she thought her father and a doctor were deliberately excluding her from a discussion about her future.

Naturally enough, parents did not want to discuss everything in their children's presence, not only to spare them from the worst possibilities but also because they needed the opportunity to clarify questions, and time to assimilate and absorb often very discouraging information before recovering the courage to support their children.

Difficult decisions

It was particularly important that parents were well-informed when choices had to be made between various courses of action. The clinical picture alone does not necessarily indicate which course should be followed. Value judgements are inescapable. What constitutes the best interests of the child is an ethical as well as a medical question, and the answers arrived at will depend on the values of the various parties to the decision. For example, when do the risks, side-effects and pains of treatment outweigh diminishing chances of cure or remission? Some parents and doctors perceive the child's welfare as best served by pursuing active treatment as long as any small chance remains that life may be extended. As two British paediatricians wrote: 'Doctors' training directs us to cure even more than to care.'[2]

Others may place the emphasis on minimising suffering and will require a greater chance of success to continue treatment. Fine judgements, requiring high standards of medical expertise but also taking into account many other variables, must be made. This issue was particularly acute when drastic treatments, such as bone-marrow transplants, were a possibility.

The parents of four of the children who had very poor prognoses recalled that bone-marrow transplants offered the chance of extending their lives for a period. Transplant entailed total body irradiation and carried the risks of catastrophic infection. Treatment might kill the child prematurely, and even if successful would constitute a reprieve, not a cure.

Two couples opted for aggressive chemotherapy and transplants. 'There were no decisions to be made, we had to give him the chance.' 'We didn't feel there was any option.' Both children became critically ill after the transplants, which were described as horrific by the parents. Particularly distressing to one mother was the pain caused by the transplant procedure itself, for which the child received no analgesia: 'The one thing I found very hard was when he was getting the transplant. He had a dreadful experience, he was screaming with pain while it was going on and I heard afterwards that adults have an anaesthetic for it.' Both young boys enjoyed a year or so of good quality life after their transplants, before they relapsed. One father remarked, showing photographs of his son looking fit and healthy after his transplant: 'To get that year, it made the treatment worthwhile.'

The parents of one of the other children with poor prognoses refused aggressive therapy, which might have extended her life but offered no hope of long-term survival. They wanted to minimise their daughter's suffering. Their decision was incomprehensible to another parent whose child, with a different form of cancer, was undergoing aggressive curative treatment. The couple decided that they would not discuss their decision with anyone else. 'We were under enough pressure without having anyone getting annoyed that we weren't trying everything. We didn't trust [people] to react by supporting us and we didn't want the hassle of an argument.' They were very appreciative of the attitude of hospital staff, who did not question their decision once taken but supported them in it. 'Surely some of the staff must have had a different opinion on the decision we took, but if they had they never showed it.' Their little daughter died six months after diagnosis.

The possibility of transplant was considered for another child but she did not respond sufficiently well to chemotherapy to allow it to go forward. She died about nine months after diagnosis.

A fourteen-year-old girl was closely involved in the decision about undergoing a transplant. Her mother and one of the doctors concerned were against it. 'I didn't think it was necessary then, she was still able to go to school. I thought it might be necessary in time.' The girl's parents felt that at her age the decision must be largely hers, but her mother was extremely critical of the lack of counselling of either the girl or her parents about the various issues involved. 'We were asked to take a decision based on a bit of hearsay. There was no counselling. These things need to be discussed in detail and in language you can understand. When you're upset you're not taking things in.' In the event, the girl died without having a transplant.

The question of transplant also arose for two boys with leukaemia. For one, it was described as 'his only hope', and the procedure was successfully performed. The second boy was doing well on chemotherapy and had a good prognosis at the time the decision had to be taken. Having decided that, on balance, the transplant did not warrant the risks involved, the parents were devastated when their son relapsed some months later: 'We were killing ourselves. Why didn't we go ahead with the transplant? We had terrible feelings of guilt that we had made the wrong decision. We were feeling so helpless about the whole thing.' Their son, ten years old at the time, consoled them: ' "Don't ever think you made a mistake" he said, "If these things happen, they're to happen".' After his third relapse in a few months the question of further treatment arose. 'There were only two options: to try another course of chemotherapy or to do nothing. They [the doctors] were really very good, it was up to us to decide. When it's one of your own it's very hard to say "Do no more". You can't say it. I don't think any parent can say it. You want to try at all costs. You never give up hope.'

A mother recalled differing views when her son was given chemotherapy after he was deemed to be terminally ill: 'The hospice people had become involved, they saw the chemo as unnecessary torture. We saw it as our last glimmer of hope. They wanted to stop the chemo and I said "No, you can't do that", believing of course that it was going to work wonders.'

A little boy with Down's Syndrome who developed leukaemia had a very poor prognosis, but chemotherapy brought a remission for some months before he relapsed. The possibility of further treatment, which might have achieved a short-term remission, but at a very high price, was discussed. His parents recalled their anguish in making the decision not to go ahead with it: 'It was a very hard decision to make but we decided that what we wanted for him was quality of life rather than quantity.'

Three other couples, whose children developed secondaries within a very short time, also remember discussions about quality of life. They were quite clear that from then on they wanted 'the least possible medical intervention'. One mother recalled a consultant saying to her: 'It's a doctor's instinct to treat and to continue, and maybe sometimes we don't take enough cognisance of what the patient has to go through.' This mother added: 'It's important to do your utmost for your child, but I think it's important for parents to be able to say "Enough

Getting information, making decisions

is enough". Parents should never lose sight of the fact that it is their child who is the patient.'

The parents of a teenage boy regretted allowing an operation on his spine six weeks before he died. They hadn't realised how close he was to death. 'I don't think we would have let them do it if we'd realised it was only prolonging his life. He went through an awful lot and it was all for nothing. They operated on him at four in the morning. When he woke up he was crying, he was in plaster of Paris and he felt he couldn't breathe. They had him on a rotating bed, he was actually looking at the floor. We had to sit on the floor to look at him. He cried for two weeks, he said "Take this off" '.

The plaster cast remained. His parents brought their son home to die.

CHAPTER 5

Looking for kindness

'All we ever wanted was kindness and support — to do their best, as humanly as possible.'

As we have seen, when children have cancer they need to be treated by experts, in order not only to have the best chance of cure, but also to minimise their suffering. But they, and their families, need considerably more than medical skill; they also need sustained, sympathetic support from all who care for them. Thus expertise should be combined with kindness, the one complementing the other.[1]

In the alien environment of hospital, such kindness is especially important. There is a wealth of evidence that hospitalisation can be a traumatic experience for children, especially the very young, and that the frequent presence of a parent is essential to their emotional and psychological well-being. Parents' own emotional well-being, or lack of it, contributes to the child's recovery or failure to thrive. Hospitals should actively encourage and facilitate family involvement, where possible treating parents as partners in care. However, acceptance of these principles is incomplete and conditions experienced by children and their families in hospitals across Europe range from the good to the appalling. Adolescents, being neither child nor adult, often find themselves in inappropriate settings: in adult wards or with children much younger than themselves.[2]

Care and conditions
Sixteen of the twenty couples interviewed for this study made very positive comments about the care and support they received while their children were undergoing active treatment in the children's cancer centre and in the ward dedicated to children's cancer. 'I don't think there was anything more they

could have done. They were first-class.'

Families came to trust and rely on the medical and nursing teams looking after their children, and built up relationships of varying degrees of closeness, with both staff and other parents. 'They just do everything, they accommodate you in every way.' 'There's a great community of us there. We still meet and support each other.'

Parents were admiring of medical and nursing skills, aware of the pressures under which many doctors and nurses work, and were ready and indeed eager to make allowances for occasional abruptness or discourtesy. For example, remembering an occasion when a doctor failed to communicate properly, a father excused him, saying: 'He's an eminent surgeon, he can't be perfect every way, maybe he just hasn't the time.'

When doctors and nurses were kind as well as skilful, and appeared to the parents to care about the children and their families, parents' appreciation knew few bounds: 'They were all very good, they were really nice, we couldn't fault them in any way.' 'We have no reservations at all about the standard of care that he got.' 'We were looked after very well, it couldn't have been better.'

When problems arose after the child returned home, parents usually went straight to their treatment centre. 'We knew they were always there at the end of the telephone, we had only to ring up, it was a great feeling.' They looked to the units for advice and support during the phase of active treatment and in some cases throughout the illness.

With one or two exceptions, family doctors and local hospitals played minor roles during the phases of active treatment, and were perceived as knowing little about the special needs of children with cancer. 'In fairness to your own GP — they don't know.'

Staff in one local hospital were unaware that children on cancer therapy are extremely susceptible to infection because of suppressed immunity: 'He got very low one day with nosebleeds [but] it was a waste of time bringing him into the local hospital, they knew nothing about it. They were going to put him in with children with whooping cough. They just didn't understand.'

However, the paediatrician in a local hospital was most supportive to one family. 'We were very lucky to have that doctor, he was very good to us and he took a great interest in the child. No matter when we rang he always seemed to be there.... I could ring him any time.'

A number of parents mentioned that their children felt safe in 'their' hospital and looked to go there when they were particularly ill or in pain: 'He would trust them to do anything, it was his home from home; if he got sick it was "Take me in and they'll make me better".' 'When she was sick and had pain and we were giving her tablets she said "I want to go back to the hospital" even though she hated hospital.' 'He had the utmost confidence in them.' 'He came to rely on the hospital, he always felt safe up there.' 'I always felt when I left him in hospital he was in the best hands, they were great to him.'

One child, who was expecting to be kept in hospital after a check-up, was 'very upset that he didn't keep her in. She was very content in there. She knew that whatever could be done for her [when she was in pain] would be done immediately there. She had great faith in them. She felt much safer there, especially coming towards the end.'

However, three families did not experience the kind of support that elicits such comments. Two of the couples concerned expressed doubts as to whether their children might have been saved if they had had better treatment. One of the children had a brain tumour. He was not treated in a specialist unit but in a general hospital, sometimes in adult wards. His parents had asked for a second opinion but the doctors 'weren't for it at all'. Since their son died, a relative's child was treated for cancer in a specialist unit and this child's care raised doubts as to whether their son had received the best treatment possible: 'We have the feeling there could have been something done for him. We get the feeling he was wronged,

Looking for kindness

but surely to God they couldn't wrong him. At the same time you just fear those things.'

A number of consultants were involved in this child's case. Although one was primarily in charge and the parents expressed gratitude for much of what he did, it was clear from their account that none of the specialists took the boy's case to heart. Some years after an operation to remove a brain tumour, during which period he was seen regularly by a specialist, 'He started complaining of a pain in his leg', and when the specialist asked him to arch his back he couldn't do it. A scan was lost for three weeks. 'The worry and tension were awful.' When eventually the scan turned up it was found that the tumour had grown and the boy had secondaries in his spine. The implications were not at that stage explained to his parents.

The boy started to suffer severe episodes of pain, but his parents found it difficult to get help. For example, they had to wait for days before seeing the specialist and obtaining some relief. When a fresh crisis arose a few days later they were told he could not be contacted because he was on leave. These parents, like others in this study, learned to be persistent. They told the hospital authorities that the specialist had said they could ring him at home — 'He hadn't of course but you'd be driven to it' — and were then given his unlisted number. The specialist said: 'I'll book him in to hospital straight away.' But at the hospital they waited for nearly eight hours before being seen by any doctor, with the boy in pain all the time. Nothing was done until the child was booked in and the specialist had been telephoned. The boy was then admitted to an adult ward. 'He was with older people who had brain tumours and a lot of old men, it was the wrong ward for him. The nurses were marvellous in a way because they were so busy.'

But the boy was in constant pain while he was in hospital, not sleeping at night because of it. His mother remembered him saying: 'When visitors are there the nurses are all over me, looking after me, but when you go away and in the night time I ring and they often wouldn't come at all.' The nurse told his mother he slept all night. 'But he told me he hadn't slept because the pain was so bad.'

Kindness was remembered with gratitude. A nurse, who later sent the boy books on his favourite sport, stayed with him during one particularly bad episode. 'He said "I'll always remember that." '

The second couple who had doubts about their child's care felt she had suffered medical neglect in her last months. Both the child and her parents had become very concerned about her deteriorating condition. This concern was not shared by the specialist, who, they found, was very difficult to communicate with. 'It wasn't that he wasn't looking after her, he was, but you couldn't get through to him, you couldn't talk to him, he was always flying low, he was always busy.'

Nor could these parents discuss their child's treatment with the other doctors involved who disagreed with the treatment the consultant had initiated. 'You couldn't talk to them because they were fighting with him.' The mother recalled alerting the consultant a few days before her daughter died: 'I said to the doctor, "She's dying", and he said, "You mean faster than you or me?", because he didn't believe she was even sick. By the next day they realised how bad she was, but this had been going on for months.' Before the child died, her mother made a complaint to hospital authorities about the neglect she perceived. The parents had attempted to call in another specialist. 'We explained that she wasn't being monitored, there was something wrong and it wasn't being sorted out and could he come back in.' If they had had another specialist, the father said, 'I could have asked him to look into it — at least they could have tried. I'm not saying they are magicians, they can't work miracles, I'm just saying they should at least listen and try. I certainly would never have felt any annoyance with the doctors if they had come to us [while the child was rapidly deteriorating] and said "Look, things are not going well, we're not sure we can do anything", but to find them ignoring you....'

After their daughter died, the parents were given little

explanation as to the proximate cause of her death. The senior doctors 'ignored us completely and left us with the feeling they didn't bother. You'd almost come to the conclusion that they let her die.'

Another family, whose child had a brain tumour, was referred from one consultant to another in what appeared to be a largely uncoordinated fashion. This couple's greatest problem was the failure they perceived of any doctor to share with them the responsibility for the child's condition. Some months after surgery to remove a tumour, followed by chemotherapy and radiotherapy, the child's condition started to deteriorate, but when scans failed to suggest a cause, the parents were left to manage the situation themselves. 'That was when the horror started. The scan was clear, but there was our sick child', who was consistently losing weight and becoming weaker day by day.

Doctors argued among themselves about what a crucial scan showed, one telling the parents the child's brain was now affected, others disagreeing, saying the scan could not be interpreted that way. 'It was like as if someone was sticking a knife into us, taking it out and sticking it in again. We had to do all the running; we had to go back to the consultant and try to get them [the various consultants] together, we had to try to get the ball rolling.' A breach of etiquette was cited by one doctor as a reason for his inactivity: a colleague had asked him to return a telephone call and he found this unacceptable.

Dealing with consultants and organising diagnostic procedures in a number of hospitals, the parents repeatedly had to drive all over the city, with the sick child lying on the back seat of the car, to organise and collect scans and X-rays, to meet doctors, often in corridors or draughty hallways. The boy's father said: 'The child was handed from one [specialist] to the other and contact was lost. I am angry, and I must be angry at all the doctors. They're all fine people in their own right, but it would seem that not one of them saw the child through. There was no one to take ownership of the problem, only us.'

Eventually this family was referred to the children's cancer centre, where they received the care they needed: 'When we went into that unit and met the doctor — if that's the care and that's the love, I really envy the people who had it from the beginning.'

Summing up their experience, this father identified what was missing in the care offered to his son, and to him and his wife as parents: 'Nothing they could have done would have changed the prognosis, I know that.... If they [the doctors] make a mistake, especially with something like cancer, we can live with that. All we ever wanted was kindness and support, for them to do their best, as humanly as possible. We wanted concern and people pulling together.'

Care for adolescents
All three of the adolescents in this study were treated in adult wards at various stages, and one, a boy whose leg was amputated, hated being in hospital, largely on this account. He 'didn't mind' being in an orthopaedic hospital, in a ward with other young people, where there was plenty of space, and indeed before going in for his amputation he had joked to his parents, playing on a word for drunkenness: 'Next time you see me I'll be legless!'

However, he then had courses of chemotherapy over a number of weeks, in a five-day ward for adults, which was located in a gloomy basement. 'It's like a dungeon, it's very dark, pipes everywhere. They were very good to him but he absolutely hated going in for the chemo because he was so sick on it. He'd lie on his side getting sick all the time, he used to hang out of the bed, and it was very awkward without his leg — I used to be afraid he'd fall.' The beds were crammed together and 'there were a lot of old men dying. A man died there one evening while we were sitting there.' The boy 'got so upset he started going hysterical. It frightened him, he was only fifteen.'

This teenager seems to have found hospital particularly hard to bear and raged and lamented throughout his chemotherapy.

Once he refused it. 'The doctor said "Do you want us to force it on him?" and we said "Yes". We had to hold him. He took a swing at the doctor, he was so uptight. Then he cried, and he cried because he was upsetting us. I think he lost his nerve, it was all hitting him, what was happening to him. He used to cry from Monday to Friday [when he was in hospital]. He wouldn't eat anything in the hospital, he thought if he didn't eat they would put him out, they'd say "He'd be better off at home". He ran out one day, with the one leg. He went up in the lift, everyone was looking for him.'

The boy's mother thought: 'He wouldn't have minded the chemo if he'd been with people of his own age.' He met and made friends with an older teenage girl who also had cancer, and they were a great support to each other, but little attempt seems to have been made to schedule treatments so that young people could be together. 'Sometimes he'd meet her going in, mostly they missed each other. At the end when he was going in, there were one or two younger people but he had no interest then.'

This boy's parents 'lived in the hospital' with him for the period he was ill, sitting by his bedside, going in during the small hours if the nurse telephoned them. They, like most of the other parents in this study, were acutely aware of how much their son needed them to be with him in hospital. As one mother commented on her period in hospital with her two-year-old: 'It was a frightening experience for me, not knowing what to expect, never mind her.'

Facilitation of parents

Almost all the children had the company of at least one parent every day, most of the day, and the majority also had a parent with them overnight.

Most of the children's wards mentioned in the interviews facilitated and actively welcomed parents, sometimes with difficulty because of lack of space and resources, and involved them to varying degrees as partners in care. However, it was disturbing to find that in some instances parents were either actively discouraged from staying with their children or were made to feel unwelcome by attitudes of staff, or by the lack of proper provisions for them.

Nurses in a children's hospital in Dublin urged the mother of a six-year-old to return to her home in the midlands; this mother was encouraged by the paediatrician in her local hospital to stay with her child, and she did. Another mother commented about the same hospital: 'At that stage [the late 1970s] they didn't encourage parents to come in [except at set hours].'

One father remarked of the cancer ward in a children's hospital that it was the only one 'with an enlightened attitude'. A couple who had brought their child to a hospital in Britain for radiation were dismayed to find on arrival that there was no provision made for them to stay with their three-year-old son: 'We realised they didn't intend us to stay and we had to sort it out at eleven o'clock at night.' By then, they said, the illness had gone on long enough for them to be aware of how necessary it was for them to assert themselves: 'By that stage we were beginning to be able to stand our ground. It is great to be able to stay with children. It is very, very important.'

The mother of a two-year-old remarked that her own mother 'wondered at me staying in hospital with her'. Another mother spent the first week of her two-year-old's hospitalisation with him, but then her own mother, who was minding the other children, advised her to come home as she had responsibilities to them as well. This mother's voice broke as she recounted how she did come home: 'I abandoned him really.' She visited him every day throughout his treatment.

Three parents pointed out that parents' presence supplemented hard-pressed staff. 'It was a great help to the nurses as well as the child.' 'The ward was understaffed. The nurses could barely do the medical jobs and feed the children, they had no time to play with them. It was a bit much to expect young children to be on the ward all day and not be entertained or kept company. The parents were absolutely essential.' A father commented on his time in hospital with his daughter:

'There was no outside world. You were always just stuck on this one corridor with all these kids that had no hair and were getting sick. It was very, very depressing, watching what they were going through. There'd be only two nurses on at night, there'd be some kids on drips and somebody else getting sick and someone else coughing and there'd be only two nurses running around.'

Eleven of the children usually had at least one parent with them overnight. Generally it was mothers who slept in the hospital, sometimes mothers and fathers took turns, and in three cases the father was the one who stayed. Often the parents slept on chairs or camp-beds beside the child's bed, either because there was no other accommodation available or because the parents' room was too far away from the ward. As one mother explained about her desperately sick eighteen-month-old: 'One of us had to be with her all the time, that's what it boiled down to. If she needed a drink during the night and you weren't there to give it to her there'd be hysterics.'

One family, which included two elderly relatives as well as four other children, lived two hours' drive away from the hospital. The parents spent long periods in the hospital with the sick child, every second day, and arranged for other relatives and friends to visit when they could not. The boy, an independent nine-year-old, used to tell his mother that she did not need to stay overnight: 'I'm well able to look after myself. I'm not a baby.'

In most cases, it was the mother who spent most time in hospital with the sick child, with regular visits from the father. The mothers wished to be with their sick children, who they felt needed them more than any other member of the family. Some of those with children in specialist units mentioned how much support they got from being in the hospital, the sense of security with known and trusted staff to hand and the solidarity with other families. As one mother said, even when she was at home all she could think of was her sick child: 'I always felt that he needed somebody there. I always felt terrible leaving, especially if he was bad, if he wasn't well and he was in bed. I can't agree with him [husband] saying that you just go up and visit him for half an hour. I just couldn't do that. I always felt I should visit him as long and as often as I could because they were all right and they were going to be all right but he....'

Another mother remembered: 'During that time in hospital I was on a constant high, I needed to get back to the hospital, to the support system; other people were suffering, we were bad and yet others were worse off. I used to feel guilty about feeling down when I came home because up there I was so high and helping others, but when I came home I had to cope with normality and I found it difficult.'

The mothers' concentration on the sick child sometimes led to tension between husband and wife. Fathers felt left out, and found the separation of the family, and the diminution of their own role, hard to bear: 'My wife got great support from being in the hospital, but I found it an enormous strain being away from her and the child.' 'I always felt most secure in the hospital, but he [the father] couldn't wait to get the child home.'

Employers generally were flexible in allowing time off for hospital visits, but as one father remarked about hospital and medical systems: 'They never really understood the fact that I had a job.' His daughter was receiving regular treatment which could be administered in about two hours, but it nearly always took considerably longer and the family was then faced with a four-hour drive home. 'If I was in the hospital with the child at nine o'clock I couldn't see why I couldn't be out by twelve o'clock. There was no reason in the world why the doctor couldn't come in and set up a drip within a half-hour of our arriving — it was routine procedure.' This father used to take time out of his holiday allowance in order to bring his daughter for regular treatment; subsequently his employer arranged time off for him. Parents who were self-employed could arrange their own time, but businesses suffered as a result of neglect.

Adapting to hospitalisation

Most of the children accepted treatment with resignation as part of their lives and adapted well to hospitalisation. Some became depressed as time passed. For example, a two-year-old whose parents thought he had 'come on by leaps and bounds' in hospital, remained 'his same sunny self' and 'adjusted much better than we did', nevertheless became withdrawn as the weeks passed. 'Instead of reacting when the nurses came into his room and the doctor and smiling at them, he would turn his face away from them. He also reacted against people in white coats, because he hated the intravenous treatment, people sticking needles in him.' The parents nervously brought the child home where he recovered his spirits.

Another boy, aged five, 'got post-radium syndrome; he was lying there, depressed, wetting, totally out of character. He wouldn't talk, he just turned into the wall.' During chemotherapy, which depresses immunity and leaves patients vulnerable to infection, this boy, like a number of others, was isolated for a period in a special room, with restrictions on visitors. Even after coming home, children had to be protected from possible infection and this boy's parents found the periods of isolation among the hardest aspects of the illness to cope with.

A ten-year-old boy who 'adapted totally, no matter what was said to him or what he had to go through he put up with it' also became withdrawn at times. 'He was going through an awful lot of isolation, it was a very small room and he was there for weeks and weeks on his own. He used to get into bad humour at times and when he did he'd turn his back to the door in the room and curl up, and you knew that day you didn't talk to him.'

Several other children were mentioned as having become withdrawn or depressed during their active treatment. One boy became so severely depressed after his transplant that he received psychiatric treatment, including drugs. Two other children were seen by psychiatrists or psychologists for one or two sessions; their parents felt these were of no benefit. An eight-year-old boy, questioned about relatives who had died, pretended to be sleepy to evade the questions, and later angrily told his parents 'I don't want that silly doctor asking me any more stupid questions!'

Quality of care

Although parents generally perceived high standards of medical and nursing care at senior levels, there were criticisms of understaffing in some wards and of the relative incompetence of junior staff. Individual junior doctors were found to be helpful and supportive, but a number of parents criticised the rotation system: 'The system of junior doctors changing every six months is a disaster. I used to feel sorry for the consultant, they're just about trained and they're gone, two more recruits come. I think in an area like that [cancer] there would be a case for keeping them a bit longer.' 'The house doctors are changing every few months, you're just getting to know one and he's moved. You get a new fellow and you go through the whole thing again.'

Children were subjected to fumblings which caused them great distress, particularly by inexperienced doctors trying to introduce needles into small and perhaps collapsed veins: 'A new house doctor couldn't find a vein, she tried his ankles, the lot, the child was hysterical. They put him through hell that day.' 'The child was black and blue. They should have people doing the blood tests who are used to it. Doctors should learn on models.'

Even apart from this lack of expertise, most of the children hated any procedure involving needles, which were a regular part of the treatment and monitoring processes. Children's fear of needles was illustrated by one little boy's reactions in hospital. Even after a Broviac (a permanent line for intravenous treatment) had been inserted, so that needles were no longer introduced into his veins for blood tests or other procedures, his fear continued: 'When the people taking blood would be passing he'd be so afraid, you'd see the worried look on his

Looking for kindness

face. I'd say "They're not coming near you, you've got your Broviac now", and you'd see the big smile. He knew he was safe.'

A two-year-old, on her way to hospital, would recognise the landmarks and begin to sniff: 'Look, Daddy,' she would say, showing the marks of injections, 'Jecks, no more jecks'. When she thought she was going home she would rush for her coat and shoes: 'The coat meant she was going home and she wanted her shoes, her slippers weren't good enough, even though her feet were swollen.'

A twelve-year-old girl was promised, when curative treatment ended, that 'there would be no more needles'. She needed a great deal of morphine to control her pain, but up to the end she succeeded in taking it orally. 'We had the syringe-driver ready but she kept it [liquid morphine] down by sheer will-power.'

Junior doctors' carelessness with hygiene caused one child and her mother great concern. The child had a central venous catheter and was fully aware of the dangers of contamination. Her mother commented: 'Some doctors don't know anything about hygiene, they don't wash their hands. They would put a needle down on the bed, they would take out the bung and leave it down anywhere.' The child 'used to give out stink, she would say "Am I going to get a bug because of this?" ' This mother added: 'Doctors should learn how to dispose of used equipment. In other words, they should tidy up after themselves.'

Nurses in general were highly praised by all the parents, for their kindness and hard work. Parents who were highly critical of their daughter's lack of care in her final weeks excepted the nurses: 'They were marvellous.'

However, one couple remembered with great bitterness nurses' apparent indifference and coldness in a local hospital where their child underwent preliminary tests before being transferred to a specialist unit where he was diagnosed. Four years later they described their experience in that hospital as one of their worst memories of their son's illness: 'Nobody ever spoke to us or asked us how we were.' Suspecting leukaemia, the child's mother 'went berserk, really, I just ran to the chapel, I nearly tore my hair out in there but no nurse came near me in all that time; the ward sister never appeared, nobody came and said "I'm sorry", and that's what I found the hard thing...these things linger on....'

Another mother found 'an enormous gap' between senior nurses and the junior nurses: 'There were a lot of student nurses and they changed very frequently. We found that some of them were anything but reliable.' Mis-timing of chemotherapy maximised her son's discomfort, causing him considerably more sickness than if the timing had been accurate. 'Nothing serious ever happened, but a lot of minor things went wrong which were quite distressing for the child.'

Hospital facilities
Most parents felt that the quality of the physical environment and facilities in hospitals was 'peripheral' or 'trivial'; what was important was the medical and nursing care. 'The things that mattered were second to none.' 'At the time you're going through it you don't think of the smaller things.'

Even when, due to overcrowding, parents had to sleep on the floor, occasionally without mattress or blanket, such discomfort was presented as minor compared with the fact that parents could stay with their children: 'The facilities were bad, definitely, as regards baths and all that, but I think when you're from the country the main thing is that you're able to stay with your child and you don't mind anything else.' 'It was cramped but we didn't mind; all you'd want is to lay your head down.'

Nonetheless, the facilities in a major children's hospital were severely criticised by a number of parents: 'The facilities were dreadful. I couldn't say anything good about them.' The cancer ward was described as cramped, drab, undecorated, the staff had to work 'in ferocious conditions — it seems to be kind of congested there all the time, it must lead to tension, but we didn't see any tension.' There was little space for doctors and parents to have private meetings. A room set aside to cater

Looking for kindness

for parents and visitors to a number of wards was described as 'the most awful, degrading place'. Even basics like heating were deficient at times. 'During the snow the heating wasn't working properly, we couldn't keep warm.' Such poor facilities as existed were mainly geared to mothers, and fathers felt awkward and out of place. One father, who lived over a hundred miles from his child's hospital, had to sleep in his car on occasions.

Also mentioned was the poor quality and presentation of the meals for the sick children, the offhand, sometimes hostile, attitude of some ancillary staff such as porters, domestics, and catering staff, the lack of such a simple facility on the ward as a kitchenette for parents to make tea or small snacks, the poor sleeping, meal and washing arrangements, especially for fathers, the fact that the cancer ward was 'the only ward in the hospital that didn't have piped TV'. It was clear that the general drabness of the surroundings and the inhospitable attitudes of some staff could lower the morale of parents under acute and often long sustained stress. 'It should be automatic in a children's hospital to consider parents. But the staff [ancillary] tended to make you feel that you had no right to be there.'

Parents were given notes to permit them to buy meals in the staff canteen, but sick children would not always be settled enough at mealtimes to allow a parent away. 'You know children — there were days I couldn't get down to the canteen. There was a rigid time for meals and if you didn't get there that was it!' 'The first day I went down to the canteen and asked for sausages, I was told "You can't have a hot meal — that's not for you, that's for medical staff", in other words "You're only a member of the public".'

On another occasion a porter refused to help a parent call a taxi to take the child to another hospital. 'These are the kind of things you could do without, you have enough to contend with. One is so vulnerable at times like that.'

The lack of thought was summed up by one mother in the hospital's failure to plant a little garden: 'There was a green patch outside the ward, you could see it through the windows, but there wasn't a shrub or a flower, not one thing to indicate there was a bit of hope around. If you could even see a rose blooming it would lift your spirits, and there were many days, as you can imagine, when we needed a lift. All parents, no matter what stage they're at, they're vulnerable, they're most vulnerable, watching their child deteriorate.'

By contrast, the physical facilities and general atmosphere in several of the other hospitals in Ireland and Britain were described as first class: spacious, freshly decorated, with excellent cooking, washing and sleeping facilities. One unit had sleeping accommodation for siblings as well as parents, and included them in all meal arrangements: 'We were fed and found.' The supportive attitude in another hospital embraced all the staff: 'They couldn't do enough for you.'

A number of parents commented that the location of a cancer ward in a children's hospital seemed to underline the plight they were in: 'It was down at the very end, for all the world like a leper colony; it looked like another planet when we went in [on the first day] and saw all the little baldy heads, it looked like Doomsday.' 'I always called it "The end of the road".' 'To me it was the last outpost.' A father said: 'I don't know if they did it deliberately, putting it at the end of a long corridor, but I thought it was the worst thing to do to people, to go down past all these corridors with all these children with normal sicknesses, right down there.... I saw all these bald-headed kids and Solzhenitsyn's *Cancer Ward* came into my head. My heart fell into my boots at that stage.' Yet this father added: 'After the first day it was the nicest, loveliest place. It was undecorated, but all the children were happy, it had a lovely atmosphere. They went out of their way to put the children first and the medicine and the doctors and nurses second. It was fantastic.'

CHAPTER 6

Cancer in the family

'Things are never again the same, are they?'

Parents of children with long-term, life-threatening or terminal illnesses face multiple practical problems. They must juggle responsibilities to the various children in the family, to each other, to household duties, to employers or employees. They also have to live with the emotional strain of a 'chronic protracted state of insecurity, not knowing for many years whether or not the child will be cured.'[1]

All of the families in my study had to re-organise their lives in various ways because of their child's illness. While parents were in hospital with the sick child, the other children in the family had to be looked after. Money had to be found to meet extra expenses. Time had to taken off work to visit the sick child or to mind the other children, and household matters had to be attended to. As one mother said: 'Something like cancer literally takes over your life.'

For some families, diagnosis was followed within a relatively short time by the terminal period, for others the illness became a long-drawn-out crisis punctuated by periods of pseudo-normality.

When children entered remission, or gained a lease of life due to transplant or other treatment, their appearance of health made it difficult for people to believe that this state might be temporary, that disease was controlled not cured. For example, having had a transplant, a five-year-old boy was 'the healthiest child in the parish to look at. He started school and you'd wonder what the other parents would think of us saying "If any infection comes into the school we have to know about it".'

Parents were placed in the cruel position of being harbingers of doom for their own children. A mother recalled that when her son went into remission for the first time his grandmother

Children's Last Days

'told everybody he was cured'. 'When we came home from Lourdes everyone was saying "Isn't it wonderful — he's cured", and I had to say "I'm sorry now, that's not exactly it", and then it seemed as though we were looking for attention. I'd say a lot of people thought we were hyping, that we were over-reacting to the whole thing.'

Anxiety about their children's health was never far from the surface, and some children played on those fears: 'He was a little trickster, he knew if he said he had a pain he would see the change in my face.' 'He was an awful tease, he'd pretend he was crying and I'd come running out and he'd be laughing at me. He was no little angel.'

A five-year-old was 'a bit of a chancer. If he didn't feel like doing something in school he'd say to the teacher: "My throat hurts me, will you drive me home?" Or he would come in to us in the morning and say "I don't feel well".'

A number of parents referred to the constant strain of the illness: 'There's always that cloud over you.' 'You're so helpless, you go from day to day, wondering is today going to be all right. That's literally what you do.' 'I was so frightened of cancer...it was taboo. When we went to St Luke's [for radiation] all I could see was people, but all I could see was dead people: that's so horrific, I was coping with all of that.' This mother went on to say: 'You're trying to think of your child but you're coping with yourself too. And there's a terrible selfishness in yourself that you don't become aware of until you're in a crisis situation. There's so much you don't know about yourself. I always felt that when my child got ill it was like someone holding a light up to my soul.'

A few parents mentioned times of near despair: 'We were on the fourth floor in the hospital and I thought "I'm going to jump out of here". I said to Sister "I'm going to hit my head off the wall". We went to pieces that day.' 'You'd feel like going in the river.' 'There was a man shot in the shopping centre and I wished it was me, because of the pain I was carrying.'

Other parents referred in a matter of fact way to the necessity of coping one way or another. As a father remarked: 'People ask you how you cope; you haven't any choice in the matter, you have to get on and cope with it.' His wife agreed: 'It's either that or bang your head against the wall, and that won't cure things either so you have to be level-headed, cope the best you can.' Another father said: 'You do what is necessary and it makes no difference, it becomes part of your normal life.' One mother remarked how much better she and her husband managed as they went along: 'It's amazing how cowardly we were in the beginning. We could face anything in the end.'

When the child was reasonably well, parents' morale was correspondingly high: 'Going through it, when they're good you're good with them and it's the best way to be, when they're down, you go down with them, and that's human nature.'

The strain was mentally and physically exhausting. A mother said: 'I was tensed up all the time, and I used to have terrible headaches because I was so tensed up.' Another mother remembered: 'I'd be exhausted because of the mental strain. I'd spend a week getting ready to go to the hospital [for check-ups or routine treatment], and I'd spend another week recovering. That's the way it went, fits and starts.' One couple were both quite seriously unwell during their son's illness, the father recovering from a heart attack and his wife waiting to have elective surgery. 'We were so tired.'

Family strains
A number of studies have been done on the effects on families of the stresses of a child's long-term illness. However, the findings of the studies are far from conclusive, and there is little agreement in the literature. Much of the early research was poorly planned and executed, with a tendency to draw far-reaching conclusions that were not justified by the evidence. Often, little weight was given to cultural, social and economic factors contributing to family problems, for example, the extra burdens imposed on hard-pressed families in countries where medical treatment has to be paid for out of

the family income.

Early research focused mainly on problems and, not surprisingly, found signs of stress, including parental anxiety and depression. However, such signs were often labelled 'maladaptive and frankly pathological', with little sensitivity being shown to the feelings and reactions of families in abnormal situations, and no attempt to define what constitutes normal behaviour in such circumstances.[2] A view emerged that families with very sick or disabled children must be handicapped families. Many people find such attitudes offensive, and evidence from recent research has discredited this view.[3]

Some studies have found little difference in marital and family strengths between families with children with life-threatening diseases or mental handicap or other disabilities, and those whose children are all healthy. The brothers and sisters of sick children often display maturity and understanding of the family situation.[4]

Unfortunately, once propagated, research findings, even if ill-founded, can have a long life. For example, the unsubstantiated view that life-threatening illness in children almost invariably leads to marriage breakdowns and emotional and behavioural problems in the children, both sick and well, is often quoted. Faced with the diagnosis of cancer in one's child, it is yet another blow to be told that one's marriage is likely to break up, and that the other children may be damaged because of it.[5]

Three of the couples I interviewed recalled suggestions made to them that their child's illness could cause their marriage to break up: 'Early on, someone said to us it can be the cause of the break-up of a family. They said it's a long hard road, you're going to have a hard time, it could put a strain on your marriage.' 'The doctor told us we had a year of hell in front of us and asked us "Do you get on well together? Because this could separate you".' The same suggestion was put to this couple in another hospital. They related these incidents without rancour and then had a desultory discussion about

Cancer in the family

what appeared to be the only disagreement they could remember throughout their son's illness, when the father had been late one evening coming in to the hospital.

Another couple remembered disagreeing about how protective they should be of their energetic son: 'I would have put him in a glass case,' said his mother, 'I would never have let go only for his father.... He would say "Let him off" [out to play], and I would say "No, no", and the tension would build up between us.' When they found out that nothing they or anybody could do would make any difference, their son could not survive, all the tension disappeared. 'We were at peace with one another.'

The mother of a child who died after a relatively short illness recalled that during the terminal phase, when the house was full of visitors and household tasks had still to be attended to, she and her husband took it in turns to be with the sick child. 'We had an understanding with each other, one was with him and the other was coping elsewhere, and there was no strain about that, no hassle.'

Another couple decided soon after diagnosis on a division of responsibilities: 'We only had two children; when she [the well child] was very small we explained that Daddy would mind her and I would mind her sister.' This mother remarked on the need to keep the father involved. 'Often the mother is so involved with the sick child, the father is left out of it.'

Another mother discussed the problems that arose in her marriage: 'I think there's a terrible strain in the relation between husband and wife. I think a mother sees nothing else but her sick child, nothing else. I think men, not that they love their child any the less, but they can switch off, and that can cause great tension between a couple.... It's just two different ways of coping. We were two totally different people coping in two different ways, loving each other but growing miles apart, loving the child but going at it in different ways and one really not fulfilling the other's needs.... [It would have helped] if someone had said that this might happen or maybe explained what was happening to us.' Late in their child's illness the

Children's Last Days

family came under the care of a specialist unit, and counselling was arranged for the parents. 'We found out an awful lot about ourselves; for the first time I had to listen to him and he had to listen to me and an awful lot that came out explained the tension between us.' This wife discovered that her husband was as worried about her as he was about the child: 'I was amazed he was actually thinking of me. I never gave him two thoughts. I could think of nothing but the child.'

The preoccupation with their sick children was referred to by other mothers: 'I became completely wrapped up in him.' Both mothers and fathers referred to the sick child as 'special': 'It's easy really now to say she was a special child but she definitely was.' 'She was special to me.' 'He was more than special.' 'I do sometimes think they're unique — or is it their illness makes them that way?' 'He was different from the others, more sensitive; he would never hurt your feelings.' A father spoke of how much his six-year-old son's courage impressed him: 'I think we underestimate a child's capacity for pain and suffering and coping.'

During the terminal period, a baby was born to one of the couples in the study, and others were conceived (four of the mothers were pregnant at the time of their child's death). One family moved house, to the delight of their sick child. Judgemental and insensitive comments by professionals continue to appear in print. A recent publication maintained that 'often the parents have a baby — the new child serving as a replacement for the ill child'. Another described having a baby or moving house during the course of treatment as 'ill-judged' and 'flights into activity'.[6] These are normal — and life-affirming — events in a family life-cycle.

One mother recalled being advised by a social worker not to become pregnant. When she found that she was expecting another baby she was embarrassed and tried to avoid the social worker on visits to hospital. The baby was born some weeks after the sick child died and 'made the Christmas for us'. Another mother felt that her new baby distracted her from her grief, and a year after her child had died her sorrow welled up and she felt overwhelmed by it.

Two other mothers were pregnant when their children died and the babies had been born at the time of the interview. One of these mothers had been very anxious that her surviving son should not grow up as an only child. As this mother was coming to the end of her child-bearing years, time was not on her side and she was very thankful to have had the third child. Another couple, who had had only two children, including the one who died, expressed during the interview their unfulfilled longing for another child.

The other children

Some households included grown-up children, or older relatives, and some had live-in help. When necessary, neighbours, other family members and friends rallied round to mind the other children, often at short notice and odd hours, as crises arose with the sick child: 'We didn't have to worry about the other children, they were brought to school, taken home, taken out to play, so they didn't feel neglected.' But as a father remarked: 'It was hard on them, all the coming and going, wondering. We had to go so fast at times with a child as sick as he was. They could be at school and we'd be gone. We always tried to let them know who was collecting them if we weren't going to be here.'

The sick child had to be given priority: 'Your whole life, everything you do revolves around the one, and the other children do take second place — but what can you do?' 'The other children were left aside for a while, but they were very good and very understanding.' 'The kids didn't seem to suffer too much from being left, they never seemed to resent their brother, they were easier on him and they never resented the fact we were with him [in hospital] so often.'

One child was 'twice expelled from the house' during her brother's illness lest he be exposed to infection. 'It was coming up to Christmas and I asked could she come home and I was told "If she comes home and he gets jaundice you'll have no more Christmases together".' Great concern was expressed by this girl's parents as to the effect this action might have had on her.

The sick children were given many toys, books, games: 'There were so many people giving him things and you couldn't tell them not to.' 'He got so many things as they all do, showered with presents. You name it they get it.' 'A lot of gifts arrived — Fisher Price garage left on the doorstep — that kind of thing.' The other children sometimes resented the sick child's privileges: 'They all rebelled, they all threw tantrums at different stages — why was he getting things and they weren't. But that was the end of that then, they got it all out of their systems.' One couple saw their well children as 'taking advantage' of the situation. The sick child's bedroom was filled with goodies, sweets, comics, games. 'They were all mad to go up and play with the new things.'

Another mother remembered the occasion when her well child realised what her sister was going through. Seeing her in hospital with a drip up 'All she could do was watch the needles. Afterwards she knew we weren't exaggerating. She really was getting a needle'.

Preoccupied with the sick child, a mother found her well children 'most demanding, seemingly totally unaffected'. She found it hard to accept that they could remain absorbed in their own affairs: school uniforms, holidays and so on.

A baby in another family became very demanding, screaming for attention towards the end of his brother's illness: 'Perhaps he was reacting to the tension in the house, although he was quite a difficult child if nothing ever happened.' Another baby, about eight months old when his brother was diagnosed, became very clingy during the course of the illness. His mother said: 'I went away so many times. That has never left his memory. He got insecure, so he hangs on to me now, literally hangs on.'

Sick children became irritable and frustrated at times, particularly with well siblings or visiting children: 'They wanted to play with his toys and all he could do was lie there.' 'He would lash out at his sister because she was well.' 'He couldn't tolerate his brother because he was everything he wasn't in terms of energy'. This child, who was in pain, was afraid of the sudden movements of his toddler brother: 'It was the unpredictability of him going for things, the darting, if the baby touched him he had pain.'

One couple regretted the demands they had made on their adolescent son when his young brother was dying: 'We expected too much of him because he was our eldest. We expected our children to love their brother as we did, and that's not the way things are at all. We didn't get the support [we needed] from our adult friends and family. Why should we expect it from our child son?' The father remembered sitting the boy down one day 'because he was acting as though nothing was happening, and I said "Do you realise what's going on in this house? Your brother is up there dying".' After the child died, the teenage boy cried and told his father that he had been frightened, he had been afraid he too would get cancer. His mother commented: 'It's very hard on the other children. Looking back now I can see it. At the time you expect everybody to know and worry the same as you do and that's not on at all. We had no right to expect of our son the things we did expect.'

A number of parents mentioned that their well children helped and supported them in various ways, both practical and emotional: minding younger brothers and sisters, helping with housework and shopping, entertaining the sick child, and through their very existence encouraging parents to keep going. 'They were tremendously supportive, they couldn't do enough for him.' 'The small ones keep you going — there's so much to do, you haven't too much time to be thinking.' 'The other children helped [emotionally]. They're there to be looked after.' 'His sister was marvellous; when she came home from school she would lift him out of the bed. He loved her, she'd chat to him, and then when she went to secondary school, the younger girl sort of took over that role. She used to sit down and talk to him, because he was blind, you see.' 'The baby was only nine months old when his brother got sick, and it was the one thing I was always glad of, he was always the same. The others didn't help a whole lot, maybe because they didn't need us, but he needed both of us. He needed cuddling and petting.'

Some couples described how they tried to prepare their children for their brother or sister's death. For example, a mother recalled that her twelve-year-old daughter had always been 'so positive' about her brother's chances. 'When I used to say to her "You know sometimes people don't pull out of it and he mightn't", she would say "Mammy, don't say that — he is getting better", but gradually, not making it too hard for her in the beginning, bit by bit, I got the message through to her that he was not getting better and we were very concerned about it.' Another boy's eight-year-old sister flatly refused to accept what she was told: 'She said "No, he's not going to die", we kept telling her but she said "No".'

School
Eleven of the eighteen school-age children were well enough to attend school after diagnosis and treatment, and three continued to attend for a time during the terminal period. School played a very important part in their lives. For one child it was a reason for living; she had attended very little primary school because of her illness. 'Before she went to secondary she wouldn't have minded dying because she had never really lived. From the day she went to secondary school she badly wanted to live. She loved school, she was determined she wasn't going to miss a day, she was mad to learn. She got eight honours in her Inter.' This teenager found it difficult to get about, being often breathless because of her disease, but she was small for her age and 'the kids used to carry her round the school. They were marvellous'.

Another teenager, whose brain tumour was affecting his sight and other functions, couldn't be stopped from going to school: 'He used to creep down in the morning about seven o'clock and dress himself in the corner of the kitchen, in case we'd try to stop him, and he'd say "I'm going now" and he'd run. His bag was so heavy and we used to say to him to wait and his brother would bring it for him, but he would never give in.'

A little boy with Down's Syndrome continued to attend his special school two days a week until ten days or so before he died from leukaemia. 'He had less absence due to illness than any of the other children who were in the whole of their health. And he loved it. He continued to make very good progress and his speech developed.' This school was a 'tremendous support' to the family: 'I could not possibly speak highly enough of them.'

School, for another child who started late because of his leukaemia, 'was the greatest joy of his life'. Staff in the treatment centre had advised against sending him to school but, aware that the child could not be cured, his parents told them: ' "We're doing it now and you can say what you like." He absolutely adored school, I never saw anyone so enthusiastic, he was thirsty for learning.' The boy's teacher read the class a booklet describing leukaemia in simple terms, and explained to them that their classmate had the disease. This teacher 'couldn't believe that he was going to die, she used to keep saying to me "Is he really going to die?" '

As long as the child was going to school, parents could hold their anxiety and sadness at bay, but when the time came that a child was too tired, or bothered by symptoms to go, the end came in sight. Thus the mother of an eight-year-old remembered: 'It was great when he was going to school. You know the way you are, everyone was in great form. Then he'd be sitting there and he'd say, "I'm not able to go." It was most difficult then.' This family lived in the country, about half a mile from the village school. 'He'd go off to that ditch across the road, and he could hear the whole school across the fields at eleven, and he'd stand up there watching until they'd go in at ten past eleven, and that went on for a few weeks. He'd say "Are the boys playing?" and he'd be wondering who was winning the races, and then he'd work at his schoolbooks until his brain got a bit slower....'

Children's Last Days

A seven-year-old attended school for most of a term after her terminal diagnosis. She was brought home from school one day because she was in pain, but 'she was very disappointed, she wanted to be in school.' The last day of term she did not want to go to school: 'At this stage little remarks were being passed on her at school, and I think she was conscious of it. She had got quite big in the tummy and in the chest and some of them asked her in school was she having a baby.' Another child's friends stopped playing with him. His mother recalled: 'He'd come home broken-hearted: "Mum, they don't want to play with me any more because I can't run".' She added: 'Once he knew I understood his hurt, that was what mattered.'

Older children were more understanding with their sick classmates. A teenage boy who was bedridden for months had visits every Sunday from his school friends: 'They kept coming and he used to be delighted that they would come...but it used to have a terrible effect on them, one of them especially...they never wanted to believe that there was anything so wrong with him that he wouldn't live.' The boy used to worry that he would have to 'use the bottle' while his friends were there, and 'if he got upset at all he'd bring on a seizure'. Other teenagers too were embarrassed by problems with bodily functions. A teenage boy tried to hide his catheter from friends; a fourteen-year-old girl needed private facilities because excretion 'was smelly and noisy'.

Passing the time

Boredom was a problem, particularly for the teenage boy who had lost his sight. 'He used to find the days so long.' His parents looked up the telephone directory to find organisations for the blind and they contacted their local branch of the Irish Council for the Blind. A volunteer came straight away. 'He thought they would never come. He said "Could you ask her to come tonight?" ' The volunteer brought craft work and audio tapes, and thereafter came several times a week. 'They were very good...it occupied his time for a long, long time. He made three baskets and a glasses case for the doctor. It made a terrible difference, any little kind of help used pick him up, keep him going.' He loved to listen to his grandmother 'talking about the old times'. The public health nurse and the chemist arranged for a well-known entertainer, who was performing in the area, to come and visit him. The boy was delighted: 'He wouldn't have his hand washed after shaking hands with him!' The entertainer 'stayed longer with him than he did performing up in the hotel, and he wrote to him and sent tapes he had made'. The boy found it hard to hear some of the tapes because there was so much laughter, he couldn't catch the jokes, and the performer sent a tape without the laughter — 'to go to that trouble'. That visit 'picked him up for about three weeks'. The public health nurse used visit on her days off: 'She'd like to know he'd be all right, she'd come up to see him and she'd bring her baby.' The GP would call 'with his own boys, and he'd think up little things to tell him, to keep him going.'

Another teenager, who had had his leg amputated, also needed occupation and stimulation when he could no longer get about. An artificial leg had been provided, but it was very heavy: 'He never got used to it, it was very awkward. In this day and age you'd think they'd provide something better. When he got the artificial leg he fell down the stairs, right down from the very top. I thought he was dead.' A member of the Irish Wheelchair Association took the boy out in a specially adapted car and let him drive it. He asked for a special three-wheeled vehicle, which cost £1000, and his parents agreed to get it for him. They also bought him a computer but he only used it for two or three days. He would ring his friend, a young woman who also had cancer and a robust attitude to life. 'You'd hear him laughing all over the house. She kept him going. He wouldn't let his dad smoke but when she came round she could smoke twenty and he wouldn't mind. As long as she sat there and talked to him he'd be thrilled.'

This teenager was big and heavy and his parents were both smaller than him, which increased their difficulties in nursing him. One day 'He wanted a proper bath, he couldn't really do anything for himself without the leg'. The family got him upstairs to the bathroom and somehow got him into the bath. 'When we put him in the bath the water all hooshed up, and the laughing of him! He kept saying, "I don't know how you are going to get me out of this bloody bath!" His brother was falling around the place laughing.' The family applied for a grant to have a bathroom, suitable for wheelchairs, installed downstairs, but the Corporation refused on the grounds that the boy was terminally ill. Months after he died officials wrote to ask if the family wished to pursue their request.

This boy became very frustrated a few days before he died. 'The children were out playing in the front and I think what really got to him was he realised he couldn't get out.... He went mad that day, he just screamed the place down and wouldn't stop. I think it was because he was in. Before he got cancer he was always out on his bike — swimming and racing were his hobbies.'

CHAPTER 7

Support from the community

'We have great neighbours, we couldn't have managed without the community.'

Many families of children with life-threatening disease have financial difficulties caused by the illness.[1] One study found that in the first week after diagnosis, half of the families in a representative group had extra expenses amounting to over half of their income; in the weeks following, the extra expenses amounted to twenty per cent of the income.[2]

A number of the parents I interviewed mentioned that shortage of money exacerbated their plight. For example, one family found money 'our greatest problem' in the beginning: 'When we were diagnosed first, having access to easy money would have helped a lot.' Travelling up and down to hospital, buying meals out, and all the other extra expenses were beyond their means: 'In the beginning we had to go looking for things and we were owing money.' A fund was set up by the local community to help meet the family's expenses, but newspaper publicity greatly upset them. It was inaccurate, embarrassed the sick child in hospital, and was, said his mother 'one of our greatest problems'. The committee dispensing the funds queried some of the family's expenses, at first 'looking for receipts', but once it was pointed out how much things cost, funds seem to have been provided without further hassle. At one stage in the illness, when the parents each visited the child separately every day, transport alone cost £170 a week.

The lack of private transport was a major problem for another family, who spent long hours waiting for buses to bring them to hospital to visit their son. The local community then raised money to buy them a car, which not only helped them in hospital visits but also gave their teenage son a great deal of pleasure as they went on trips all over the city and county. The boy was an excellent swimmer and very early one summer morning his parents drove him down to Dollymount strand and helped him out of the car. A man on a tractor was cleaning the beach and when he saw the boy's artificial leg being removed 'he nearly ran into us'. The boy 'didn't care that morning. He just wanted to get into the water'.

Another couple, who paid for private treatment, had to sell their car. Their small business declined because the husband could not devote enough time to it. 'We lost so much work, we were absolutely broke really.' A year after their son's death, when the interview took place, they were 'only now beginning to pull out of it'. At one stage their teenage son, who was on steroids, developed a voracious appetite. 'In four days alone, between biscuits and coke, not taking account of sandwiches or cereals, we spent £74.' The family ran an account with the local shop, which was how this particular sum was recorded. 'It would have to be real Coca-Cola. He would notice the difference.'

Other families, while they played down the extent of their difficulties, mentioned how the accumulation of expenses, and the loss of earnings, had set them back: 'We're only getting sorted out now.'

Parents' attitudes to the financial costs of the illness were similar to those expressed about hospital facilities. Money spent or debts accumulated were trivial compared with the enormity of the child's illness and death. Thus a mother said that her husband gave up his job because he found it very difficult to spend enough time with his daughter in hospital. 'The way we looked at it was, she came first before his job. If we'd no money we'd no money.'

Expenses
Three of the fathers left their jobs and went on social welfare to enable them to spend time in hospital and help look after the family. 'We couldn't have managed otherwise.'

Support from the community

Three of the mothers also left employment, taking temporary leave of absence in each case. One of those mothers had been advised by doctors to 'go back to work and keep everything as normal as possible'. She did so but became exhausted and regretted afterwards that she had not taken leave at an earlier stage in her child's illness.

A young couple, whose only child died, said they had no extra expense at all, the medical and drug expenses were met by the state, and 'we'd be minding her anyway'. Five other couples, all from professional or managerial backgrounds, said 'money was the least of our problems' and mentioned how glad they were to be able to pay for what was needed, including extra help, without worrying about expense.

A family at the other end of the economic scale adopted the attitude that their sick child came first and 'hang the expense'. 'We spent nearly all our time and all our money on her.'

Such responses echo those of parents in studies of families of disabled children and of children with life-threatening illness, interviewed in the UK, who also gave a low priority to the financial costs of caring and considered a word such as 'sacrifice' to misrepresent their feelings.[3]

A number of couples mentioned receiving financial help from grandparents, brothers and sisters and other relatives. A few received help from hospital and children's cancer funds. Local community fund-raising was also an important source of finance for some families. Without such assistance they would have found great difficulty in managing, particularly if they lived any distance from their treatment centre: 'It was very expensive going up and down to hospital. Without the community fund we'd have had a serious problem; once the fund was there, there was no problem.' 'We spent more money! I don't know how we survived — money we didn't have, but it came, people gave it to us, our friends, our families. People were super to us, they really came up trumps.' In a poignant aside this mother added: 'We were extravagant while he was ill, we did things we wouldn't normally do, to comfort ourselves.'

Medical, nursing and hospital fees

Medical fees, drug charges and hospital expenses were met in most cases either directly by the state through medical card and other entitlements, or through the Voluntary Health Insurance scheme (VHI), which covered most, but not all, of the costs incurred. One family, who were not in an insurance scheme, paid for private treatment. The costs of treatment overseas were met either by insurance schemes, local health boards, EC schemes, local voluntary fund-raising, or from a combination of sources.

Difficulties in obtaining entitlements were mentioned by four couples. Medical cards for two children were refused initially on the grounds that parents' incomes were too high, but were subsequently issued. Two fathers recalled arguing with health boards over the funding of treatment overseas, and another had a disagreement with the VHI. Another father found his local health board 'outstanding — I couldn't give them more praise, especially the chief medical officer. Virtually anything we wanted, they arranged it'. This family was greatly worried when their child was put on special treatment costing over £100 a day: 'There was a question over whether or not the VHI would pay. In fact it was worse than that: they [the doctors] didn't want the VHI to pay because they wanted to set precedents [for health boards to meet the costs of such treatments]. I was so worried about that one day, I couldn't even think about the child. As it turned out the health board paid. It was the same kind of thing with the transplant. No doctor ever said "Don't worry about the money, we'll sort that out". We were told to go to our TD. "Wasn't he great."' In the event the transplant did not take place. The health board involved in this case also gave contributions towards the cost of regularly travelling hundreds of miles to and from a Dublin hospital.

Another family stated that: 'Community care [the local health board] paid for an awful lot of stuff. We couldn't in our wildest dreams pay hundreds of pounds a week for morphine. We were fortunate that they understood the situation.'

Two families had night-nursing services paid for by the Irish Cancer Society, but there was some misunderstanding in one case, which led to considerable worry for the parents: 'The hospice said we should have a nurse one or two nights a week, they said we'd be allowed a nurse for seven nights. We got all mixed up, I'm sure it was the doctor took it up wrong. They would allow a nurse for five nights but that was only if the person was dying. It came to £625 in the end and there was absolute havoc over it. The GP in the finish had to go to the Lions' Club [voluntary group] to pay some of the nurses.'

A hospital bed was supplied for a teenager whose leg had been amputated but the wrong sort was delivered: 'It was just an ordinary hospital bed with a rest but no pulley — he needed something to pull himself, just to inch himself. We were lifting him, but the pain....'

Likewise it took a fortnight to locate a special buggy for a child who had to keep his leg straight — the doctor thought a bone was fractured — by which time the child was too weak to use it.

Domiciliary Care Allowance

The majority of the families received the Domiciliary Care Allowance, a discretionary, non-means-tested payment to families caring for disabled children at home. Some were told about it by their hospital social worker, the remainder found out about it in a variety of ways, including from other parents. One mother was given the application form by the public health nurse who told her 'not to tell anyone else, not to be telling everyone my business'.

Another family attending the same unit was not receiving the allowance and this mother told them about it. They applied for the allowance and belatedly received payments. Both families were interviewed in this study and the mother of the second family commented: 'I find that none of these social workers, in the hospital or in this area, will tell you what you're entitled to. It's very difficult to make out why community welfare officers have that name. They're supposed to be for the welfare of the community, but if you suggest to them you might be entitled to something, they'll tell you they don't think you qualify for it, so you're automatically thrown out, and then you discover afterwards if you press it, it's there.' This family lived two hours drive from the hospital where their son was treated; his mother often travelled by bus at a cost of £14 return. The child was in and out of hospital for over three years, but his mother only found out about the allowance a few months before he died, and received payments only from the date from which she applied.

Another mother was told about the allowance at her local child health clinic. A few couples, including those attending the same units as families receiving the allowance, had never heard of the allowance at the time of the interview. Inconsistencies in the award of a similar allowance in the UK, with only a few parents applying successfully, caused great bitterness.[4]

A number of parents in this study were distressed to be sent payments after their child had died, even though they had notified the relevant authorities of that fact.

Two families mentioned the home help service provided by health boards. In one case the public health nurse arranged for a home help to assist the family: 'She came twice a week, and she was lovely. She was a lady who had lost a child herself and she was very sympathetic, and a very fine person.' In the second case the mother said: 'I was looking for a home help, trying to keep the housework going and looking after the kids and up and down to hospital; I can't remember what happened but we didn't get the help.'

Pilgrimages and religion

Fund-raising was a practical way for the local network of family, friends and neighbours to demonstrate solidarity with the sick child and family. This support and concern was perhaps most vividly symbolised in the organising of pilgrimages to Lourdes. 'The pilgrimage to Lourdes is an occasion for the symbolic act of charity, an elaborate form of practical assistance.'[5]

Sixteen of the twenty children in the study visited Lourdes, and in four cases the pilgrimage was a gift from the local community. The spirit in which such gestures were offered and accepted can be seen in a father's use of the word 'hospitality' to describe what was given. A neighbour sounded him out as to whether the family would be offended if something was organised by the community, or if they would accept it. The parents felt it would have been discourteous to refuse, and in any event the gesture was for their child: 'In the first place, we wouldn't have been able to bring the child to Lourdes ourselves and we felt what we were doing was we were accepting the hospitality on the child's behalf.' A fund-raising dance was arranged and the mother remembered: 'We hadn't to do a thing about it. I hadn't even to bake a cake, I felt so guilty. We got the tickets for Lourdes and I even got spending money.'

A GAA club raised money for another family to go to Lourdes: 'They said they wanted to do something and they said they'd send one of us [the parents], but the response was so enormous the whole family was able to go. An anonymous donor even gave £500 spending money. We took all of that, we weren't a bit proud. Some people would be very independent and send things back but we didn't. I felt it was marvellous and if people wanted to do it we appreciated it.'

While no doubt some of the families hoped and prayed that their child might be cured, the reasons why people go to Lourdes are more complex than the search for a miracle: 'Cure was incidental to the main purpose of the journey.... The pilgrimage fulfils a need in the lives of those who are seriously ill' (and, it could be added, their families) 'which is overlooked by medical treatment. The sick pilgrim' (or grieving parent) 'feels better, not in the sense of receiving a cure — that occurs in only a tiny minority of cases — but in the sense of feeling stronger and more reconciled to their lives.'[6]

The parents who talked to me said little about the actual trip to Lourdes, but it was clear that at the very least the parent and child, in a number of cases both parents and all the children, had enjoyed their trip to France.

One couple's child deteriorated very badly during the pilgrimage. The visit still brought a kind of healing. These parents had felt unsupported by the medical profession, and their friends and family seemed not to understand or truly care, but in Lourdes 'for the first time we had support'. The people in their pilgrimage group 'opened up their arms to us and couldn't do enough and were not afraid to be involved'.

Four of the twenty children were not brought on pilgrimage to Lourdes. One of the couples concerned brought their little boy to Knock. The three other couples saw pilgrimages as irrelevant to their needs. One couple did not believe in religion, a second expressed the opinion that 'if he was going to be cured he'd be cured anywhere'. The father of the third child said: 'I'm not very religious. I go to church but I don't believe in it. I wonder why I go, I don't disbelieve in it, it's my own mixed feelings, like most people I think, if they would only admit it. I have no problem believing in God and all that part of it, it's organised religion I don't believe in.'

Some parents mentioned that their religious faith was a source of comfort to them during their child's illness and after the death. A mother said: 'I have tremendous faith, and when I have trouble I just storm heaven for the strength to help me cope.'

A few couples referred to regular Masses and Communion in the home. One family noticed such an improvement in their child after he was confirmed that 'We really thought the miracle had happened'. However, one father had a crisis of faith after his son died, and a few parents mentioned feeling let down and not believing in anything any more.

Most of the families interviewed had expected their local priest to offer some form of pastoral support. Priests who had shown concern by calling on the family and offering prayers, and particularly by keeping in regular contact, were praised. Thus one family said approvingly: 'The priest called every night', and another remembered a 'jolly priest' who used to call and sit on their teenage son's bed and make him laugh.

When priests did not call or express concern about the family's ordeal, they were felt to have failed in their duty. A mother said bitterly that their priest did not call until requested to do so. 'I said to the priest who did come in the end, "[Even] if you hadn't two words to put together, you might not have the gift of the gab, you might not know what to say...but that doesn't matter — come and be there — that's what matters".' On the other hand, the couple who did not believe in religion did not welcome their priest's regular calls.

Priests were not expected to provide answers for the family's suffering or to produce theological justifications. Families looked to them as to doctors and other professionals, and family, friends and neighbours, to express concern and to be alongside them in their time of trouble.

A hospital chaplain was particularly helpful to several families. In one case he struck up a friendship with the sick child whose parents could not visit him every day. In another he intervened most helpfully on behalf of a suffering child. The chaplain in another hospital failed a mother who wanted to be reassured that her child, whom she recognised as being less than perfect, would none the less go to heaven. 'He just told me to have hope.'

A number of families mentioned their own, or their child's, attachment to relics, including holy cloths and Padre Pio's glove. Three mentioned bringing their child to faith-healers; none was much impressed. Their attitude could be summed up as 'you'd try anything'. Two others contacted a faith-healer by telephone, and a mother remembered: 'I just felt that somehow, without saying it, she was telling me that he wasn't going to be cured. From that moment I slowly started preparing myself.'

Community and support

The need for emotional and practical, as well as financial, support from family, friends, neighbours and clergy was repeatedly stressed by many parents: 'We couldn't have managed without the community support.' 'If we'd been left on our own, I think we would have cracked up under the strain.' 'I do know that support was vital.' 'Unless you had family near you, you'd be lost.'

Without such support one mother felt very much alone: 'All I wanted was for someone to be there, or even just someone to ring up and say "How are you?". It didn't happen from the people I wanted. There were terrible long, lonely months when no one would ring. There was terrible isolation.' When at last this family came under the care of a specialist unit and the parents were asked how they were coping, 'We couldn't answer except to cry, because somebody actually asked, somebody cared.' One couple, who described themselves as very private people, remarked: 'The way people rallied round was great, but we were never invaded, our privacy was respected; phone calls, letters — we appreciated the support, the people were saying "We're with you", the support was there if we needed it.' Another couple welcomed constant company: 'We have great neighbours. From the last time we brought him home from hospital we were never really left on our own, there was always somebody with us.'

A mother said she had dreaded being left on her own with her daughter, who was failing fast, lest a crisis arise — her other children were at school, her husband at work — but without anything being said to her, her neighbours kept her company. 'The local ladies — there was always someone here — as soon as one left by the front door, another came in at the back.'

Similar tact was shown to another family by a friend who asked could she do anything. The child's father wordlessly gave her his daughter's best clothes, those selected for her burial. 'She laundered the dress, bought new socks and underwear, she was terrific, she did a beautiful job, she was terrific because she just did it and didn't ask any questions.'

A few couples mentioned that gifts of ready prepared meals were very helpful: 'The nuns sent out a dinner for us one Sunday. We hadn't eaten for a while. They sent plates of salad

Support from the community

prepared just to pop into the fridge and use as you needed and a lovely cooked ham and bread. It really came in very handy because it meant that both of us were able to eat and be in with the child.' Another young couple mentioned that towards the end of their child's illness they 'lived on chips', and their GP offered to make a casserole for Sunday lunch.

But sensitivity was lacking on many occasions. Some families had too many visitors, who had to be given hospitality and who outstayed their welcome. 'When the child was sick we were inundated with visitors, coming morning, noon and night. Some of them had very little cop-on.' They would stay for hours, while the mother excused herself to look after her child. 'Some of them would come, have a cup of tea and then they'd go, but there were the few who couldn't do anything to help.' At times visitors stayed until the small hours, adding to parents' exhaustion. In rural communities, especially, families would be wary of giving offence by being less than welcoming on all occasions. One family who lived out in the country did not feel they could 'hold visitors at the door' as might be possible in a town. 'When they had made the effort to come out here....'

One mother remembered being advised not to tell too many people her child was so ill but, as she said, when neighbours asked how he was she could only tell the truth. Another couple recalled that visitors 'used always to come at the wrong time, I used to feel. At night time we used to get no sleep much, but at ten or eleven I could get the chance to sleep, but there would always be somebody there and they might stay until two in the morning. Now I often feel sorry for not telling them to go home, but you see you'd be so worried about insulting people.' One father was so exasperated by an inquisitive neighbour that when she asked for the umpteenth time how was the child (then in a terminal coma) the father snapped: 'The doctor says she has a bad cold and she's to get up out of that, the bold girl!'

A constant visitor to one family 'was the type that would always like tea to be made and that you'd make a fuss. It was nice to see people coming but it was too much at times.' Other visitors were more practical: 'My sister used to come down every day but she'd never want tea or to be made a fuss of, she'd just go ahead and do the washing up or whatever had to be done.'

Ambivalent feelings about visitors were mentioned by one mother. 'There were too many people here a lot of the time, we never really had an afternoon to ourselves, and we were so busy anyway, the time seemed to go very quickly. Probably the very moment you wanted to be on your own somebody arrived. And yet if nobody came, nobody cared, so really it's not easy.'

CHAPTER 8

Terminal care

'The saddest day in all her illness was the day we brought her to hospital and she got no treatment.'

At least four of the twenty couples were aware from the time of diagnosis that their children would die within a few years at most. Other couples had periods of gradually diminishing hope, when relapses became frequent and treatment was no longer effective. For a few families, however, the terminal diagnosis seems to have come unexpectedly, without any intervening phase.

The first relapse, for some parents, was as bad as, or worse than, the initial diagnosis. The mother of a ten-year-old recalled: 'He had been so well, flying around, up on the tractor, we had been to Lourdes...to tell him he was relapsed was something else.' This boy's Hickman line was removed before the results of his routine bone-marrow test had been received. 'I'll never forget his face. He lifted up his gown and said, "Mum, it's gone, I'm rid of it."…. Knowing I had to tell him it was going to have to go back in again before that evening was out…. He was sitting up eating sausages for his tea…. I can still see his face, he had the sausage on the end of the fork [when he was told], it stayed between his teeth and then he just dropped it on the plate.'

For one couple, the end of uncertainty after the cycle of remissions and relapses was 'initially almost a relief: it was something we were waiting for anyway'. Some parents found the terminal diagnosis even harder to accept than the initial diagnosis: 'It was much harder to reconcile ourselves to a death sentence the second time around.' 'For the first time there was no hope.' 'That was the very worst time of all. I think our world fell apart.'

Other parents said the original diagnosis of cancer remained the greatest shock in all the illness. A couple who had opted for life-extending treatment for their child, whom they knew could not be cured, agreed with each other: 'The initial diagnosis was the worst shock, a nightmare. Looking back at it, the second blow wasn't as bad as the first blow.'

A mother whose daughter had nearly died after major surgery but then appeared to make a good recovery said: 'Maybe we'd have accepted it better if she had died when she was really sick than when she came on so well.'

In a number of cases the diagnosis was given unequivocally and there was no question of further treatment. 'He said they'd tried everything available for her. He said, "There comes a time when it could not be justified, we wouldn't be treating the child, we'd be treating ourselves. All we can do now is discontinue treatment and let nature take its course."' 'She told us there and then that it was back in the same place and six months was the outside of it.' 'The doctor sent for us and told us he had six months to live.'

However, the parents of a child with leukaemia who had relapsed a number of times in a few months were faced with two options: 'To try another course of chemotherapy, or to do nothing.' These parents opted for further treatment for their son.

The terminal diagnosis

At the time of the terminal diagnosis most of the families were in the care of specialist units and good relationships had been built between them and the treating teams. A number of parents expressed sympathy with the doctors at having to deliver the terminal diagnosis: 'I felt sorry for him, he was so disappointed, he thought he had her.' 'I really felt for him that day.' 'It's terrible such wonderful people have to be the bearers of such bad news.'

But the pattern of poor communication and lack of support, which had begun with the initial diagnosis, continued for two families of children with brain tumours. 'We were sitting there from ten o'clock until half past five [waiting to have a brain scan read by a neurosurgeon]. It wasn't the doctor's fault, he was in theatre all that time. When he did come he had two or three nurses or doctors after him and he began to talk about the child in front of him. I said "Excuse me, do you mind if we go outside?" It was another corridor job.' The surgeon told the parents he thought the child's brain was affected, and that he had six to eight weeks to live. The child's mother said: 'I had to turn away, because I was choking, I couldn't talk, I couldn't listen, I couldn't let these people see my grief.' The second family had little privacy either. 'It was visiting time; there were people up and down the corridor.' The parents and teenage son 'were standing there and the doctor said to us "You know your son is dying of cancer".'

Such approaches contrast with the skill and sensitivity with which a doctor and his team prepared one couple for their child's eventual death: 'The fantastic thing about them was that they brought us from where we were, very slowly, expertly. They didn't remonstrate with us, they sort of gave us something to hope for and slowly took it away.'

Taking it in

Many of the parents recalled that it took some time for them to absorb fully the terminal diagnosis and to accept it in the sense of believing it at an emotional as well as an intellectual level, and some did not accept it.[1] One couple pushed the thought of their child's death 'to the back of our minds...we just didn't want to think of the inevitable at that stage. It probably takes a long time to accept it, to come to terms with it.'

A father whose child was quite well for a period after the terminal diagnosis said: 'It took about two months to sink in. We brought her home here and she was flying around the place, up to her usual devilment. When you'd see her in the morning going out to school on her bike, you'd begin to wonder "Is somebody kidding us? She can't be going to die" — that's what we found very hard when we were told she was going to die.'

Some parents said they 'just didn't believe' the diagnosis;

others resisted it: 'She told us not to build up our hopes that she would live...but I was putting that to the back of my mind, I didn't want anyone telling me.' 'You try to deny so much, you don't really want to know.' 'The hospice people really tried to tell me that he hadn't long to live but I wouldn't listen. I had heard so much at that stage. I didn't want to know. He was lying there for six weeks and we still expected him to get up and walk.'

However much some of the parents accepted intellectually the probability, given medical evidence and experience, that their child would die, hope mediated reality. Most parents hoped to the very end that their child would be saved — by new treatment, by spontaneous remission, by a miracle however defined: 'Our child was going to die, there was no doubt about it, but we always had hopes, we hoped to the end.' 'No matter how anyone tries to prepare you, you keep hoping beyond all hopes that it won't come to that. She did improve, and I thought there could be a miracle for our child.' 'You always hope, even though the doctor explained that this last treatment wasn't a cure. While they're doing something you hope, you think maybe they'd hit on something that will work.' 'I felt while we were in hospital there was hope, while there was something being done there was hope.' 'You're preparing yourself but you don't give up hope.' 'I suppose we were looking for a miracle, as I suppose everybody does. We had a few little irons in the fire, various people praying and all the rest of it.'

Such hope may well fulfil the essential function of sustaining parents and enabling them to support their dying child. The delicate balance between realism and optimism, and the manner in which it shifts over time, was captured by a mother who remembered when the realisation came home to her: 'I think the moment of truth comes, it was a very specific moment. From then on I was slowly starting to prepare myself for his death, before I had been preparing myself for a miracle.'

Terminal care

Preparations

Some of the couples I interviewed had been advised by a social worker to make arrangements for their child's funeral in good time.[2] Their reactions to this intervention were mixed: 'She was great; she said the time had come to organise everything, to pick out the clothes, to talk to the undertaker, so we had everything organised. The undertaker was a nice man. Only for somebody came and said it we'd never have thought of it on our own. All we had to do was go to the funeral. I don't think we would have handled any of that [so well] without her, so on the whole I think it was very good. But every time she came I found it upsetting because it brought the death nearer.'

A mother remembered: 'She was very helpful in a way we didn't realise at the time. On her very first visit she talked about his death. I really thought that was heartless and cruel, I thought awful things about her that day to have made us go through that session — "Have you thought about where you'd like to bury him etc". I think it was too soon for us and more than half of us didn't want to believe it or fully accept it; we were still in the miracle stage, so she brought a cold dash of reality. I think we were pushing that to the back of our minds, we were just getting on with our daily routine, hoping for a miracle. We just didn't want to think of the inevitable at that stage. It probably takes a long time to accept it, to come to terms with it.'

A father recalled: 'When the social worker came there was no pretence or softness, she hit me straight down the line, "You've to organise the funeral".... My folks were away at the time and I thought "Oh, my God". We had each other, and our daughter, but you need a little bit more, I think, at that stage...it frightened me a terrible lot.' This father was out at work while his wife nursed the sick child: 'It brought the whole thing in to me, to be told so early was very hard.' But the young parents were glad they were prepared because 'the funeral just went click, click, click, and by the end we were so exhausted'.

Another couple remembered: 'It was "if" anything happens to her, but then the social worker came and said "Have you decided what will happen when she dies?". We were choked, we couldn't speak, we'd thought about it privately, but we hadn't discussed it with each other, we couldn't.... When she was gone we decided we weren't flying in the face of God by discussing it, and in five minutes we had it all decided....'

Other couples made their preparations unprompted: 'We had everything done, the grave picked, the coffin ready, so we had no hassle at all. We thought of it ourselves, we thought of it a long time, that was part of our preparation, getting ready for the whole thing.'

Nine of the children were relatively well for a time after the terminal diagnosis; they continued to enjoy childhood pleasures, including birthday parties, bicycle riding and visits to the seaside. Three of the children attended school during this period.

While children were reasonably well, families continued their routine lives: 'We tried to keep everything as normal as possible.' 'We kept going, we always went for our drink, we didn't just sit down and say "She's going to die, what are we going to do?"'

One couple brought their son to the United States to see a specialist introduced by their own consultant. The trip brought no hope of cure. Although the boy was well enough to visit Disneyland, both he and his parents were so devastated by the gravity of his situation that their enjoyment was slight.

Other children were already very ill by this time, suffering from many different symptoms including pain, breathlessness, constipation, weakness, headaches, and paralysis. Most of the other children developed similar distressing symptoms in the course of their illnesses. This was by far the greatest problem experienced by a majority of these children and their families during the terminal period.

Terminal care
People with terminal cancer, and their families, need skilled

symptom control and emotional, psychological and spiritual support. They need to know that they are valued, will not be abandoned, and will be accompanied to the last.

Dying children's needs are very similar to those of adults, although they are often met in different ways.[3] Their greatest need is for a sense of security, which most often comes from their parents. As the great exponent of hospice care, Cicely Saunders, said: 'A child separated from its mother may be quite safe, but it feels very insecure. A child in its mother's arms during an air-raid may be very unsafe indeed, but it feels secure.'[4] It seems that dying children who are not in acute pain or discomfort, and who feel loved and secure, may not be particularly distressed psychologically. 'There may be a tendency to think of these children as more upset than they, in fact, are.'[5] Remembering her dying sister's last days, a ten-year-old remarked: 'She wasn't that sad.' Younger children often die very easily.[6]

Adolescents, however, face particular difficulties, and the plight of dying teenagers is especially poignant. Old enough to fear death and to resent the ending of their short lives, on the threshold of independence from their parents but forced through disease to be dependent again, they face a double crisis: their transition from child to adult and from life to death.[7]

The aim of good terminal care must be to achieve the best quality of life possible for the dying child and family in their own unique and changing circumstances. The severity and difficulty of the child's symptoms, the social, medical and nursing supports available to families, the family's own wishes, strengths and weaknesses, are all factors that must be taken into account.

There is a consensus that terminally ill children should be cared for at home if possible.[8] Children like to be in familiar surroundings, nursed by their parents with their family around them, and there is less disruption when all can be at home. Parents, who are often made to feel helpless and excluded in hospital, are in control in their own homes and the family's privacy can more easily be maintained. All of the members of the family can be involved in this most profound of family events, instead of some, as often happens, being left outside while the trauma unfolds elsewhere.

However, the idea that home is best for dying children can result in misplaced emphasis on the location of care and death. It can lead to parents feeling pressurised into taking their children home from hospital, or that they are failures as parents if their child dies in hospital.[9]

If home care is to achieve comfort for the child and family, a great deal of skilled assistance is usually needed, and this is not always available. Families may be left ill-equipped to cope with the often frightening and fast-changing symptoms of advanced cancer. A proportion of patients have exceptionally difficult symptoms, which are easier to control in hospital or hospice.[10]

Some families abhor the thought of a death occurring in their home. Others feel safer in the familiar security of the ward or unit where their child received treatment. Terminal care should be part of these units' services. Flexibility is the keynote: the child's condition and other factors can change, sometimes very rapidly, and the system must be able to respond accordingly.[11] As Colin Murray Parkes argued: 'Home care should not be seen as an alternative to in-patient care but as part of a package of services which will usually include both.'[12]

All but three of the children included in this study spent most of the terminal illness at home. 'The best thing we did was to bring her home — she cheered up immediately.' 'Once he wasn't in hospital he didn't care.' 'It was the best for all concerned if we could have him at home because we could all be with him without any big pressure.'

The parents of a twelve-year-old girl who was paralysed, 'completely helpless', for the last six weeks of her life had decided, when they brought her home, that 'whatever way we managed, she was not going to go back to hospital because I knew she had really had enough of it at that stage.' A seven-year-old girl who died in hospital was most anxious to be admitted as her condition deteriorated.

Parents, especially mothers, who had the main responsibility for care, remained heavily dependent on professionals for help with, and advice on, nursing a dying child. Before the child returned home, as one father put it starkly, 'To develop this tumour and die', the hospital staff typically instructed parents, to varying degrees, about symptom control, and assured them that they could return their children to hospital at any time, either to the treatment centre or to a hospital nearer home. In a few cases the specialist team contacted staff in local hospitals to inform them about the child in case of emergency admission. For most families, the treatment centre had been a source of security throughout the period of active treatment, and contact was maintained after the child returned home, although the nature and frequency of contact varied, ranging from occasional phone calls to regular visits to the centre.

Some consultants gave their home telephone numbers to families, and several called on the families in their homes. The family of a teenage boy with a brain tumour had little contact with the treating consultant once the child was at home: 'There was no back-up service from the hospital; only for the GP and public health nurse, we were forgotten about.'

Three families continued to look mainly or entirely to their treatment centre for care, and contacted the hospital if problems arose; they made little mention of GPs or public health nurses. All three children concerned were admitted to hospital because of distressing symptoms and died there a day or so later.

Most of the children spent periods in hospital during the terminal illness, mainly because of episodes of pain or other symptoms. One child spent some weeks as an in-patient in a hospice before returning home for the remainder of her illness.

Clearly, when children were in hospital, the major responsibility for their physical comfort rested with hospital staff. 'They're out of your hands then,' remarked one mother. Parents in some instances acted as partners in care, nursing their children and acting as advocates when they perceived care to be inadequate. One of the two children who spent most or all of their terminal illnesses in hospital spent his last weeks in and out of hospital as his condition deteriorated, while the second spent eleven weeks in hospital before his death. (See Table 1.)

TABLE 1

Location of terminal illness and death

Location of terminal illness		Location of death	
Mainly at home	17	Home	14
Mainly in hospital	3	Hospital	6
Total no. of children	20		20

Fourteen families were largely reliant on GPs and public health nurses, in eight cases with assistance from hospice services. (See Table 2, page 95.) One child spent some weeks in a hospice before returning home for the remainder of her illness.

Some GPs were perceived as 'marvellous', and became as much family friends as professionals: 'He was always a caring kind of person and I think they're the people that get caught, because if they give you care at all they wouldn't walk away from the situation.' Others were regarded as adequate; a few were felt to have let the family down. For example, one mother said: 'The GP knows so little, he never came near us for months. He said "Ring me if you need me". I could have rung a doctor every single day. I said it to them. [One doctor replied] "Do you think we can call on all our patients like that?" I said, "Do you really have an awful lot of children dying of cancer?"'

Public health nurses varied too. Some were highly praised,

TABLE 2

Services mainly relied on by parents

GPs and public health nurses	14	With hospice home-care	6*
		Occasional hospice home-care	1
		Hospice in-patient	1+
Local hospital	1		
Treatment centre	5		
Total	20		

*One child died one day after hospice home-care was introduced.
+A hospice offered in-patient, respite care, to another family 'so that we could have a holiday', but the child's parents would not consider being parted from him. Another hospice offered in-patient care to a teenage boy, but again his parents preferred him to be at home with them.

being constantly available and supportive to families: 'She was the type of person who would help anybody no matter who they are, she was always ready to come at any time.' This nurse cooked special dishes for the sick child, and even though she was on leave, looked after him one day so that his parents could attend their daughter's Confirmation. Others were dismissed as 'useless — sure she knew nothing'. 'She was no help really, she'd come in with the coat and the gloves on, she would never touch him, she would never go near him, she'd say "Well, you'll manage now yourself", and go away again. She used to keep telling me [mother] "You need a nurse, you're not getting any sleep".... It used to be so frustrating that they'd be worrying about me. I'd need help but I didn't know what I was looking for.'

One night-nurse 'used to sit down and do her knitting'. She would go home in the morning leaving the teenage boy in a wet bed. 'I would have to take him out of bed and wash him and change all the clothes...[at night] she would come down and tell me he had wet the bed and I had to go and change it. She was being paid £25 a night and I was still up...the nurse was causing problems in the end.' A second night-nurse was better: 'She was very good, she would stay awake all night with him, talking to him if he couldn't sleep. He was mad about her.'

A number of mothers said that they would have welcomed some advice on home nursing: 'I never cared for anybody that was sick like that before.' 'I would have welcomed some tips on home nursing...maybe there were things that would have made it easier on the child.'

But too much advice could be confusing. One mother was told to 'watch' her bedridden son's back and to 'keep him up straight in case he'd get pneumonia, and in the finish I used to be listening to so many things I thought my head would burst'. No one explained why there was concern about the boy's back. 'When I'd say "What'll I watch?" they'd say, "Watch that it's all right." I was expecting something to grow out of his back, that was the idea I had.' Then one morning his back 'was kind of black. It was a pressure mark. It was just a bedsore.' A nurse advised them to leave it alone, not to treat it, but as the child's mother said: 'It would have spread and it would have smelt and everything.' The sore healed after two months of treatment. Another child, who was paralysed, also developed bedsores but her mother said she could feel nothing and was not distressed by them. She died soon after.

Hospice care made a crucial difference to seven families, relieving the children's pain and supporting the parents. In the eighth case of hospice involvement, the team was introduced to the family the day before the child died, too late to offer real support.

Three families mentioned how helpful and efficient their local chemists [pharmacists] were, supplying drugs promptly and out of hours when necessary.

Table 3 on page 97 draws together, in summary form, the

TABLE 3

Parents' assessments of effectiveness of health services during the terminal period. It is striking how varied the families' experiences were, suggesting a lack of consistency and reliability in some areas.

[Children 1-20]

Ch.	GPs	Nurses PHN/other	Hospices	Treatment centres+	Local hospitals	Chemists
1	v.good	v.good		v.good	poor	v.good
2	good			good	good	
3	fair		v.good	v.good		
4			v.good		poor	
5				v.good		v.good
6	fair			good		
7	good			good		
8	mixed*			mixed	poor	
9	fair			mixed		
10	poor	poor	v.good	good		
11			too late	mixed		
12				v.good		
13	v.good	v.good		mixed		good
14	v.good	good	v.good	mixed		
15	good	good			mixed	
16	mixed	mixed	v.good	mixed		
17				v.good		v.good
18	good			mixed	v.good	
19	fair	v.good	v.good			
20				mixed		

+Treatment centres: the hospital regarded by the parents as having the major responsibility for planning and giving care. This includes the children's cancer centre, the children's cancer ward in a general hospital, and the adult wards where the teenagers received treatment.

*Mixed: this category is used when parents assessed some aspects of a service as very good and others as poor.

parents' views of the support provided to the families by the health services. Each family's experience is listed separately; if they did not mention a particular service or did not say what they thought of it, no entry is made.

What was very clear from the interviews was the need for a proper systematic approach to care, with twenty-four-hour availability of skilled help and advice. Forward planning is essential. As Kathleen Murray, nurse specialist in palliative care, has written: 'A lot of our time is spent anticipating problems that may arise, alleviating them before they happen, and preventing a crisis that may upset both patient and family.'[13]

However, such support was not available to some families I interviewed, who repeatedly referred to their fear and isolation: 'We were so isolated, we really needed someone to consult, someone here all the time. We could have done with someone like the ward sister [from the treatment centre] here.' These parents were very frightened to be told that their child might develop tumours 'all over the place' and one might push his eye out of its socket. The child's mother was horrified by this possibility: 'I said it to them in the hospital, I wouldn't have allowed it to happen.' Another mother said: 'The fear was the worst, the fear of what might happen.'

A father worried throughout his son's terminal illness, which lasted for over a year, that his kidneys would fail: 'That was my greatest anxiety during the whole of his sickness. We were so far from the hospital and we were facing into the winter....'

Inability to contact doctors or nurses, especially during crises of pain and at weekends and holidays, was a cause of great stress. Worse, the lack of a systematic approach to symptom control led to extreme suffering by some children.

CHAPTER 9

Pain

'This poor body has suffered so much.' Twelve-year-old girl dying of leukaemia.

During the long illness, the greatest problem for many of the families I interviewed was the pain endured by their dying children. Most people with advanced cancer have severe pain, and this includes children. This pain can be relieved without undue difficulty in up to eighty per cent of cases, using drugs alone. The more difficult types of pain require more sophisticated treatment, but considerable relief should be possible for all but a tiny proportion of those dying of cancer.[1]

Truly intractable pain in advanced cancer is rare and is nearly always due to inadequate use of opiates.[2] New understandings of the deployment of pain-killing drugs (largely due to the hospice movement) mean that the principles of effective drug relief are easy to learn. For instance, doses should be tailored to the individual patient, not standardised. They should be given at regular intervals to prevent pain from appearing, and should not be held back until the pain has 'broken through' and become unbearable. This is the reason that the common practice of prescribing drugs to be taken PRN or 'as required' often results in poor pain control. Dosage and timing of drugs should be constantly monitored and adjusted ('titrated') to suit individual patients' changing needs.[3] An advantage of this approach is that once pain is under control it is sometimes possible to reduce opiate doses.[4]

Side-effects of opiate treatment, which invariably include constipation and sometimes nausea, should be anticipated and controlled. Constipation, in particular, is often neglected and can shorten life.[5]

The risks of breathing problems, tolerance and addiction, which are often quoted as reasons for withholding opiates from patients in pain, have been greatly exaggerated. When terminal care is properly organised such risks are minimal.[6] These principles apply as much to children as to adults.[7] Children metabolise morphine in essentially the same way as adults, and need doses in proportion to size.[8]

In spite of all that is known about the relief of pain, it is estimated that as many as one third of people with advanced cancer suffer severe unrelieved pain before they die. Ignorance, failures of organisation, over-emphasis on acute care aimed at cure, and cultures which appear to be willing to accept avoidable suffering contribute to this failure.[9]

Degrees of pain

Pain is a complex feeling, with both physical and emotional aspects which interact with one another. There is no instrument to measure the extent of pain and indicate the appropriate response.[10] It is, after all, at one end of the highly personal spectrum of feeling. 'Sensation in general has pain as it were buried into it.'[11]

Fear and loneliness may evoke the sensation of pain, whereas excitement or distraction, or the restoration of a sense of security, can lessen it. Thus soldiers or games-players in the heat of activity may feel little or no pain despite serious injury, while a frightened child may experience agony from a finger prick for a blood test.

Some pain is functional, operating as a warning to move away from a fire, for example, or to stop doing something. Chronic, persistent pain, especially when a person is dying, serves no purpose.[12]

Psychogenic pain, that is, physical pain that is solely psychological in origin, is rare in people dying of cancer. In an analysis of the causes of pain in 100 patients admitted to St Christopher's Hospice it was found that in no case was it psychogenic, although often the pain was heightened by depression and anxiety. In any event, pain is no less real when its cause cannot be identified: the first duty should be to relieve the pain even if the pathology is not understood.[13] Children and adolescents suffer disproportionately from the tendency for their pain to be labelled psychogenic.[14]

Pain in children has long been ignored and misunderstood. Misconceptions abound.[15] Melzack, an important theorist of pain, wrote: 'It comes as a terrible shock...to find out that our ideas about pain are dominated by the myth that children do not feel pain as intensely as adults and therefore require fewer analgesics or none at all.'[16] The long-held theory was that the immaturity of children's nerve ends results in less feeling.[17] Not only does such a belief run counter to most people's experience — childhood is full of pain, as children learn that the world is a dangerous place — but also there is considerable scientific evidence that children feel more pain from similar pathologies than adults and that the younger the child the lower the pain threshold.[18] Nonetheless, it seems that surgeons continue to perform lengthy operations on infants without anaesthesia.[19] There are a number of reports of neglect of symptoms and pain control in dying, injured or post-operative children.[20] Children with second and third degree burns to seventy per cent of their bodies received one dose of aspirin.[21] Melzack commented that such 'outrageous statistics are found in virtually every study that examines the treatment of severe pain in children'.[22]

Textbooks on cancer in general, and children's cancer in particular, contain very little on the relief of children's pain.[23] The nine most used paediatric medicine textbooks in North America contain a total of three and a half pages, out of 15,742, on pain and its management. There are similar examples from other countries.[24]

The partly subjective nature of pain certainly poses problems for assessing and then treating children's pain, especially in the very young. Children often react differently to pain than adults. For example, they may hide or deny their pain, to avoid injections or swallowing foul-tasting medicine. They may not connect the relief of their pain with the taking of medication. They may not realise their pain can be relieved. Sometimes they have lived with pain for so long that they do not remember what it feels like to be pain-free.[25]

However, although children (like many adults) may not be able to describe or localise their pain in precise medical terms, a number of simple but effective tests and tools to assist in assessing children's pain have been devised.[26] When children have advanced cancer it may be advisable to assume the existence of pain and intervene accordingly.[27] In particular, children can become sensitised to repeated painful procedures such as injections or lumbar punctures, so that pain becomes worse each time.[28] Where pain is severe it is better to overestimate its strength than to work through a range of drugs before relieving the child.[29]

Dying children frequently suffer from a multiple of changing symptoms besides pain, such as breathlessness, bleeding, seizures, bedsores, fungating tumours and others, all of which, without prompt, expert care, can cause a great deal of distress.[30]

All of the children with cancer in my study experienced pain caused by advanced disease. This pain was moderate to severe for all except two of the children, whose pain was mild and well controlled. Six children had moderate to severe pain which appears to have been fairly well controlled; their parents did not emphasise episodes of uncontrolled pain. Eleven children suffered severe, inadequately controlled pain, in six cases while in hospital. In four of the hospitals this pain occurred after the children had been admitted specifically for pain control. Three couples mentioned that constipation and bowel movements caused their children great distress. (See Table 4 on page 103.)

1 Mild to moderate pain, controlled

The two children with mild to moderate pain were cared for at home throughout the terminal period, which lasted approximately six weeks in one case and six months in the second. Their parents had been instructed about symptom control, equipped with morphine and oxygen and given training in how to administer it. The families also had the help of their GPs and public health nurses and maintained contact

TABLE 4

Assessments of the children's pain and how well it was controlled. (This table includes only the children with cancer.)

1) Pain mild to moderate, controlled	2
2) Pain moderate to severe, controlled most of the time	6
3) Pain severe, out of control at times	11
Total	19

with the treatment centre, but no crises arose. 'The actual distress was minimal, and the morphine controlled the pain.' 'We gave him morphine, but he needed minimal doses. Twice, maybe three times he had to get morphine, he wasn't in any pain, he just wasted away.'

2 Moderate to severe pain, controlled most of the time

A twelve-year-old girl wasn't able to sleep in hospital because of pain. 'Once we came home, she went on the morphine. She had no problem with pain once morphine was given to her regularly.' The public health nurse and GP called every day, but 'she wasn't interested in them at all, anything that had to be done it was Mammy had to do it and that was it.' Hospice home care was offered but the child did not want any more strangers coming in at that stage. 'We didn't seem to have any problems, really, everything was done for us.'

Three of the children were very young when they died, less than three years old; they indicated by their behaviour when they were in pain, or the level of pain was increasing. One child 'became very uneasy', another's parents just 'knew by her' when her pain was increasing. Analgesia was increased or strengthened accordingly. One little boy was given Calpol, then Ponstan, and morphine in the last few days. The family was in close touch with the treating unit, and a hospice home-care team was also involved.

One of the two-year-olds 'took a turn' one day and her mother resumed giving her morphine. She had stopped after a friend, a nurse, had told her that the morphine 'made them pass on quicker'. 'I said I won't give it to her unless she's in pain and I know she's in pain but it got to the stage where I had to give it to her, she was in pain.' This child resisted taking the morphine by spoon and her mother had to 'force it through her teeth'.

The parents of a little girl who went into a coma for the last weeks of her life had been instructed on pain control by the consultant in the unit. He was available by telephone for advice at any time. The child was initially on Ponstan but was changed to morphine in due course. These parents commented that once they were at home: 'It was up to us then.' They titrated (adjusted) their child's medication as they thought necessary, waking up at night to give it. Their GPs, public health nurse, hospice home-care nurse and chemist were immensely helpful. 'The health service did us proud.' Their daughter was up and about for around five months after the terminal diagnosis, then she lapsed into a coma and died three weeks later. Their GP called twice a week to begin with, then twice a day towards the end, and came during the night. The hospice nurse was 'very kind and very skilful'. She would come on her days off, but the parents sometimes found her unforthcoming. For example, the mother asked one day why the child's gums were bleeding, but 'she wouldn't tell you anything, she was more like a doctor, you know the policy of doctors — tell the patient nothing.' They had to wait until the public health nurse came and explained. 'It was silly really,' remarked the child's mother, 'we were looking after her.'

This couple felt that their public health nurse was the best help of all. She was always available and treated the parents as partners. 'She would tell us what was going on each day, she was blunt and open.' The consultant in the specialist unit had sent the child's file to the local hospital in case of emergency and arranged for the parents to meet the local consultant. 'He wasn't a bit nice. He gave the impression that he didn't like the children's hospital.' The parents found him 'very condescending' and were irritated by his attitude, 'generally telling us what to do and he hadn't a clue himself. I got the impression we were a nuisance to him, that our daughter would be one less of the proletariat to worry about. He just didn't seem interested.' Apart from that, said these parents, 'We got the best of everything.'

The parents of a five-year-old had been told 'fits might happen and to give him morphine if he had pain, as he needed it, not at regular intervals but as he needed it'. Although he 'never complained', they knew he had pain when he 'tensed up and clenched his teeth', and then they gave him morphine. One day 'he just roared and stiffened up and I couldn't get the morphine in — he couldn't open his teeth.' His parents were frightened and decided he would have to go to hospital 'because they can inject him or treat him'. Before they left for hospital the child 'was all chat' and wanting to have a second bowl of cornflakes. He died in a coma a few days later.

A teenage boy, who was on regular morphine, only once asked for extra relief. His mother said: 'When I thought about it afterwards, he was in pain all right. He used to lose his head. He used to scream at me for different things and then he'd say "I'm sorry, Mam". If you touched him or lifted him he'd get annoyed.'

3 Severe pain, out of control at times

An eleven-year-old boy in final relapse of leukaemia 'had terrible trouble with his anus, and that gradually got worse, the pain was terrible.... They [hospital staff] could never really make out [what was causing it], there was no point in probing at him, it was just a matter of relieving the pain, but when he used have a bowel movement he'd cry.' A week or so before he died, 'He was walking around but he was uncomfortable, he wasn't eating as much which meant there weren't so many bowel movements.' He was in considerable pain; tablets he was given 'didn't seem to relieve it an awful lot'. He resisted going back to hospital: 'Definitely he should have gone back on the Saturday, but he wouldn't and I didn't want to upset him.' He died in hospital and during his last few days was on a continuous drip of Omnopon.

Another eleven-year-old boy with leukaemia was suffering from heart failure due, his mother thought, to the radiation treatment prior to a bone-marrow transplant. The doctor encouraged the parents to keep their son at home as much as possible: 'It ended up that we brought him home, but if we thought he was worse we could bring him back.' The boy had trouble with his breathing and had to sleep propped up. 'It was frightening to see. He'd lie down and try and breathe, and then all of a sudden he couldn't breathe on his own and he'd sit up. He couldn't sleep because he was terrified.' The leukaemia came back and the doctor explained subsequently that 'on account of the transplant it came back really strong, it was like wildfire going through him'. The last week, which was spent mainly at home 'was very bad because he had an awful lot of pain. It was in his joints, his knees and his back. He was so bony. He used to get very frustrated because of the pain. He used to cry "Why me? Why am I suffering like this?" ' His mother said she wasn't able for this. 'I'd panic with him, and then I was getting short-tempered with him because there was nothing I could do. If he said he had a pain anywhere I was kind of cross with him. I would say "Look, I gave you your medicine so it can't be too bad" — that was a kind of a cover-up because there wasn't anything else I could do. One day he had fierce pains in his knees and I'd given him his Ponstan and it wasn't working and he wasn't able for it. I just didn't know what to do.... I used get so mad that I couldn't do anything for him.' The parents brought the child back to his specialist unit where he was given morphine and died a day later. 'He should really have been on the morphine a lot sooner because that really helped him. The last day he was a lot happier because he was on this morphine.'

A five-year-old boy's pain was controlled 'fairly well; we had three bad episodes. [One day] I had just given him his Ponstan

Pain

and quite suddenly he got this terrible pain in his side and it went to his head.' This family had the help of a GP and public health nurse, and occasional calls from a consultant from their treatment centre. The child was started on morphine. He 'got terrible constipation, he used to sit on his potty and cry and cry. When it came to the constipation it was trial and error, most definitely. I don't think doctors are very good at dealing with constipation.' The child's father said: 'It was terrible to see this poor little fellow, so sick and so low, having to go through this terrible discomfort and crying. It was terrible to think that it couldn't just have been nice and easy for him....' 'The worst thing' said the child's mother, 'was the constipation and the fear of pain. Maybe he didn't have the fear of pain but I did. Coming up to Christmas I was thinking, "If he has severe pain, what if I can't get anybody?" He had fierce pain in one of his legs and the doctor said there was a bone broken — he had to keep his leg straight. Two weeks before he died he said "My knee hurts so much" and literally begged for anything that would relieve the pain.'

A seven-year-old was well enough to go to school for a time. She was given pain killers 'as required' but would not say she was in pain. Her mother remembered: 'She wasn't one to tell you she was in pain, but it always showed in her face, it would get flushed on one side and I'd know she had a pain.' One day her teacher brought her home from school because she was in pain. 'The next day I gave the tablets to the teacher and said if she took the pain to give her one of those and that was fine.' However, this child's pain increased and the tablets she had been on (Ponstan) 'didn't seem to do any good'. Her parents brought her in to their local hospital where she was given morphine for the first time, but nothing seemed to work. 'They could not do anything for her, they gave her everything, they rang the children's hospital looking for advice, she was clinging to the bed with pain. That was the worst time she had,' said her mother. After nearly twelve hours, 'She literally conked out from all the stuff they had given her.' Her pain was never allowed to go out of control again. Later when this child was on regular morphine, taken by mouth, and spending most of her time lying on the sofa in the kitchen, 'She might tell you she had a niggly pain, it might be a severe pain but she would tell you it was niggly.' She was fully aware of the need to take the morphine regularly. 'If five minutes elapsed from the time the morphine was due she would eat you.' At one of her regular check-ups 'She was flushed...all her features changed'. The doctor told her mother 'She was deteriorating very fast and did we feel happy about having her at home. There was no problem about bringing her back to hospital if she got worse. I was afraid of what was going to happen and that I wouldn't be able to mind her....'

The child returned home but was very weak. A few days later 'She kept saying that she'd love to sigh, but she couldn't do that, and she couldn't breathe, and you could see her heart pumping very fast....' It was decided to bring her back to hospital and 'she sat up the minute she heard that'. On the way to hospital 'we had to go very slow, the least little bump that day was very hard on her. We had to stop about six or seven miles from home and give her the morphine on the road, the sweat was pouring off her.' At the hospital the doctor was waiting. 'I don't know what he gave her but whatever he did relieved her anyway; and he sat with her for a long time. She was able to breathe, and she was able to sigh, as she said.'

A four-year-old boy was also initially given Ponstan for pain. After a few weeks his pain increased and his parents brought him into the local hospital, where staff failed to give him relief. 'They had no idea of the pain he was in. He was on a small dose of morphine, they were giving him little sups, and saying you can't have any more for four hours, and in an hour and a half he was rocking with the pain; he was in pain for three days, he couldn't sleep. They were going by the book. At one stage a junior doctor said he was taking him off morphine altogether. He said he had wind. I said "That's not wind, that's the tumour growing."' The child's father got in touch with the treatment centre consultant who contacted the hospital doctor and advised him to ' "Double the morphine, treble it,

Pain

the book goes out the window." He said he shouldn't have any pain, there should be no need for pain at all.' This young boy's father commented: 'That was the worst part of his treatment and diagnosis for the couple of years he was sick. That three days of pain. Everything else couldn't be avoided, but that three days of pain should have been avoided.'

A hospice home-care nurse accompanied the family home from hospital. 'She was great, she took over really from there.' The child was given oral morphine for four or five days, then a syringe driver (a battery-operated device which delivers small doses of morphine every few minutes) was fitted which kept him comfortable for the remaining five days of his life. 'He didn't want any more needles, but it was great, it kept him at a nice level, kept him nice and easy. He was snoozing all the time, really.' The minute the hospice nurse walked in 'you'd feel the peace in the room, you knew everything was under control. It was as she said, the pain was controlled'. This nurse cared for the family for many months after the child died, being a regular visitor to the family at the time of the interview.

An eight-year-old boy 'used to take this little pain, we had a tablet for it and it used to cure this pain he'd get'. His father remembered wondering whether their child really needed his tablets every four hours and telling him 'every tablet you do without is a victory for yourself'. But 'there came a time when he needed it all'. One hot Sunday the pain suddenly increased and 'the tablet was absolutely useless'. The GP could not be found and the parents brought the child to their nearest hospital, an hour's drive away. There, said his father, 'the trials really started'. 'All the child wanted was an injection to cure the pain. I told them he had a tumour but it made no difference, they had to get the papers out and the files down and go through everything. They wanted the discharge papers and they couldn't get through to the GP.' Finally they gave the child an injection. 'He was kept in for three or four days that time and the pain never left, owing to not having the proper tablet or injection.' This father commented: 'We were ordinary people who were never used to serious sickness. We should have been told that there will come a day when [Ponstan] will be no use — "You will need this stronger stuff, have it on standby" — they should have known. We were let down by the medical profession at that stage. They knew that the child was going to get worse and worse. Along with the development of that tumour he should have had a programme of stronger drugs. The only crib I ever had in his sickness was not being prepared, being let down that Sunday, because it was a harrowing day. Looking at the little fellow roaring in my arms, us running for help...the other children went wild....'

A nine-year-old girl, whose tumour was 'taking over her body' developed 'pain she couldn't stick. I brought her to the hospital and the student doctor put her on two Ponstan and told me to bring her home. We gave her the Ponstan but she still couldn't stick the pain, so I brought her back and they kept her in.' This time the consultant was contacted and the child was given morphine.

Another child's pain went out of control during a pilgrimage to Lourdes. He had a brain tumour and was on steroids to reduce the pressure in his brain. 'The first day we got to Lourdes the pressure rose and rose so that he had three excruciating days.' There were four or five doctors in the pilgrimage group 'but they were all GPs and they wouldn't let me increase the steroids — now common sense told me to do it.' Eventually the child's father succeeded in contacting the specialist back in Dublin and 'all he said was "double the steroids". We've often pondered how he could have let us go so ignorant to Lourdes: he should have told us in the event of another attack to double the steroids. The child came back a cripple from Lourdes.'

Three children suffered unrelieved pain in their specialist units. The parents of one child said: 'We had a bit of a wrangle for the first few weeks [after the child was admitted for terminal care] as to how much [analgesia] he should get and that kind of thing.... Once when he was in dreadful pain, someone on the staff suggested that they send up to the hospice and ask for the doctor there to come and advise on

Pain

pain control, but the consultant nearly went crazy at the idea.... Anaesthetists were brought in on the situation and they did devise a kind of regimen to control the pain and they did eventually get it right. Now it took a fortnight.' But another crisis arose: 'One morning he got into dreadful pain, they think he haemorrhaged into his spine, he was screaming. I was crying, the nurse was crying, it was pathetic.' The child was on a continuous infusion of Omnopon: 'They switched it up, which didn't seem to be ever effective, fast enough and that didn't work.' 'The hospice weren't involved at all, the paediatrician wouldn't hear of it. I think there's something lacking; I'd like to see it changing, if you haven't the expertise in one area and if you're big-minded enough you'll call in another person who has the expertise. These things should never have presented themselves; it was dreadful to see him in pain, dreadful.'

A twelve-year-old girl was sent home with Ponstan as the analgesic while her pain was 'not severe', but then the pain increased and more Ponstan was prescribed. Staff in the specialist unit suggested to her parents that their anxiety was contributing to the child's pain. A junior doctor said to them: 'I know you're very fond of her and that's why you are telling her she has so much pain.' The parents began to think perhaps they were right and at home they tried to persuade the child to last longer between painkillers, but because the pain intensified she had to return to hospital. There the child 'climbed the walls with pain on occasion'. By now she was being given epidural analgesia but 'the nurses would tell her she only got an injection two hours ago and that it should do for six hours. It would only be when she was in really dire straits that they would ring for the anaesthetist to come down. Sometimes he wasn't available.'

The child's father was 'browned off' at that stage 'with people telling me she had no pain. She would cry and sob with pain. The doctor said that some of it was psychological, not that she hadn't pain but that she was blowing it out of proportion. I had said to them that she woke at night with the pain, crying with the pain. You don't wake out of your sleep with psychological pain.' They tried a placebo, injecting water rather than a painkiller, to see if the suggestion to the child that she was getting a pain-killer would lessen her pain. Usually the child 'got almost instant relief — three minutes and she'd say "that's grand".' The water was injected. The child was 'entirely pain at that time but delighted it was going to be gone in a few minutes'. But it didn't work and the child was 'terrified. She had got this and it didn't work and she wouldn't be getting anything else for another six hours'.

The anaesthetist was called. 'He took his own sweet time to come that time.' Now the child's parents were desperate. 'We'd tried everything.' Some months previously there had been suggestions of involving a hospice but no progress had been made. The child's father rang the hospice, received warm encouragement, and soon after his daughter was admitted to the hospice.

'From that moment the pressure went. They were absolutely fantastic. They had her room ready for her, beautiful flowers and everything. There was no more "I gave you a tablet an hour ago", they believed every word she said. If one tablet didn't work they tried something else. There was no such thing as telling her "It should work". They wanted her to stay a few days so they could establish the pain threshold, which they did.' The hospice had a pet budgerigar and the young girl was given the job of bathing it. 'The bird bath was as good as ten MST tablets: the experts, you see. The hospice doctor was absolutely fantastic. He'd come in and sit down and talk. He might open up a book and say "Who's your favourite pop singer? Is it Madonna, the blondey one they're all talking about?" If you didn't know, you'd be wondering when he'd be getting to looking after her, or asking some pertinent questions, but all the time he'd be sizing her up. He had so much time for her — there was no rush. If it was important to her, it was most important to him. The pressure evaporated: on the child first of all, then on me, then on my wife and the family and the house. It's an awful shame she had to suffer

Pain

before we found out about the hospice.'

The child returned home in due course and came under the care of a GP whom her father described as 'an extension of the hospice'. She visited every day and was in constant contact with the hospice. Not only did she spend a great deal of time with the child, but 'she supported us' said the child's mother 'in such a way that it enabled us to keep going; she spent as much time looking at the way we were reacting to the situation as she did looking after the child; she encouraged us when we would feel desperate or wondering if we were doing the right thing. She was there, she was a steadying influence, she was marvellous.'

This couple's confidence as parents had been badly shaken when doctors labelled them over-protective and suggested they were contributing to their daughter's pain, through their own anxiety. By contrast, the GP, said the child's father, 'used to make us feel a million dollars, she would say "Ye are wonderful parents." Sometimes we would think the child would be better off in hospital and the doctor assured us she would never have been as good in hospital as she was at home here because of the way we were looking after her. But we were backed up by the loveliest, the most loving team that God ever put on earth.'

When a teenage boy developed secondaries to a brain tumour the specialist informed his parents he would die within three months. He also said: 'All I can tell you is that he's really going to suffer and he's going to have an awful lot of pain.' This prognosis filled his parents with fear and dread. The boy lived for over a year, cared for at home by his parents with the help of a dedicated GP and public health nurse. 'While he was in hospital he was in constant pain; it would be up to the doctor to say they could give him a 10m injection [of morphine]. They'd say, "That's all you're getting now for another few hours." If you thought you weren't going to get it the pain would get worse, you'd have it in your mind, that's what I used to find.'

The boy said to his parents: 'They [the doctors] stand at

the end of the bed, all this old doctors' chat the way you wouldn't understand it.' He felt the doctors were talking among themselves but never actually talking to him. 'If you happened to be awake,' he said, 'they might ask you how you felt, but they don't care about my pain and they're not giving me any explanation for it.' The parents were then told they would have to take the boy home: 'They [the doctors] said they couldn't keep him in hospital for ever: ''You'll have to learn to do the injections yourself.'' We came home with steroids, MST [morphine tablets], laxatives, and within two weeks of coming home he was on 150m of MST, four or five times a day. But then he was constipated and his mouth was sore.'

When doctors allowed the boy home they 'said to come back in three weeks' but they thought he would be dead in three weeks. 'Once a person they say they can't do any more for, goes home, they don't know any more about him.' The boy's mother tried to arrange a hospital appointment because 'he used to be crying and crying to go back up to the hospital' because his pain was very hard to control and he wanted relief and an explanation for it. 'He used to count the days and say ''I'm going up on such a day'', and of course we had no appointment, nothing. When they wouldn't see him that gave him the feeling that there was no more to be done for him.'

'Only for the GP and the public health nurse, he was forgotten about. They were absolutely marvellous; in a way they had to be, because there was no one else we could turn to.' The boy 'trusted the doctor an awful lot. No matter what happened, he felt that he was going to make it right. He'd never come in and rush away, and we were never under pressure about him coming as a doctor. He used to bring his own lads to see him; he'd have different things to tell him, he'd work it all out...he made so much of him, he became very involved.' Once when the GP was away they had had to call another doctor who 'didn't show any interest'. The boy was vomiting and had pain (it transpired that he had kidney stones which the family doctor and mother treated themselves). 'All the locum doctor said to me at the door [when he was leaving] was: "What could you do for him bar cart him into town in an ambulance?" — he meant into the local hospital. I will never forget that. He could have said "I wish there was something I could do for him" or something....'

Some months after the boy came home, this family discovered that there was a hospice in the same city as their son's hospital, about fifty miles from their home. The home-care team visited, advised on pain control and supplied a syringe driver. Initially the GP or public health nurse changed the syringe each time but then the boy's parents did it themselves, waking up during the night to do so. 'If we had known about the hospice sooner it would have helped a lot.' Before that 'We were really lost. You could give him injections for ever and the pain wouldn't go. The pain he used to get was like labour pains, the sweat used to come out through him...it would die out for a few seconds and then it would start again. It used to start in his leg, up along his leg, and all one side of his face — you could actually see it in his face.' The boy's mother commented that the specialist in the hospital 'should have sat down and told us all the things that would happen. He should have been able to tell us the problems that would be coming up, and put us in touch with the hospice.'

From time to time the parents were advised to cut down the dosage of morphine. 'We'd cut him back a bit but then we'd have to build it up so much again to get on top of the pain, we'd be up and down and it would take a while to get it right again.' The boy 'was terribly afraid lest anything happen to the syringe driver — he depended his life on it'. On a short visit to hospital for a scan, not long before he died, staff disclaimed all responsibility for the syringe driver and morphine. 'They didn't want it inside the hospital' said the boy's mother, 'I had to be responsible for it. One of the first things they said to me was "We're not going to be responsible for anything." We felt really that he may as well have been a leper. A doctor said about the syringe driver: "I don't know will we take that off or not — you shouldn't be using that in the hospital here because people will think they should have one." But a lot of the nurses were very interested because they could see he was in terrible pain, they were affected by it.'

The boy was extremely anxious about his condition, especially when he began to lose his hearing as well as his sight. 'He was really frustrated. It took a lot of drugs to quieten him down. He woke up like a monster really…. He couldn't hear us or see us and if you'd catch him, straight away he'd panic because he didn't know what you were going to do…. When his hearing went he was in an awful state. He couldn't figure out what was wrong and we couldn't answer him.' He was given Atavan. 'It was supposed to relax him when he was so upset about these things' but he got a 'terrible false strength. It took five of us to hold him down, he'd come out of his sleep like a bear.'

The boy's hearing returned. 'We used to keep talking to him — that's how we found out he could hear.' Then he explained to his parents what he had been feeling and thinking during the months when he was deaf, as well as blind and semi-conscious. 'He thought he was in this place like a dungeon; he was so thin the bed used to hurt him; we had sheepskin rugs under him but he thought they were made of steel wool and he said the feeling against his skin was terrible.' He thought everybody was against him. 'He was so afraid.' When he could hear again, 'He started to put the pieces together, he used to laugh about it then but he said how terrified he was.'

CHAPTER 10

Last days

'She put her hand back on my hand on the wheelchair and said "Thanks, Da".'

In the days before they died, many of the children in this study indicated to their parents and others that they knew what was happening, thus settling anxieties about what and how to tell them about their future.

Relatives and professionals alike often look for guidance on whether to tell the children their diagnoses and prognoses and on how to respond to questions children may pose.[1] This topic was raised by many of the parents I talked to. Each child and family is unique and the dynamics of the unfolding situation are subtle and complex; there are no universally applicable recommendations, although much emphasis is placed by experts on honesty and the importance of listening.[2] Twycross and Lack welcome recent trends towards truth-telling but warn that 'evasion and deceit must not be replaced by total candour...[which] can be dangerous and not infrequently damages patients' and families' coping mechanisms.'[3]

The often posed dilemma of 'to tell or not to tell' implies omniscience on the part of doctors and ignorance on the part of the patient. It also fails to take into account the importance of non-verbal communication, to which children are particularly sensitive. While doctors may be sure that an illness will be fatal, they can rarely predict when the death will occur. Many children, like adults, come to an awareness of their condition without being directly informed in words.[4]

Good communication with dying children about their condition is less a matter of giving information, still less of thrusting it on children who have not asked for it, than of attentiveness to what the dying child is seeking to elicit, convey or ignore and responding with sensitivity and support. It involves neither drawing a 'curtain of silence around [the child's] most intense fears' nor applying 'the dogma of always divulging truth'. Children themselves often set the pace, choose whom to question and confide in, and open and decisively close discussions.[5]

Some patients, adult or child, may try to avoid the whole subject of their condition. 'They wish others to take over all responsibilities, anxieties and decisions.' This protective role is natural to parents, and is one that some children encourage; for example, a nurse asked a twelve-year-old girl, dying from cancer, did she worry about her condition: she replied 'I leave the worrying to Mum and Dad.' This child discouraged discussion of her treatment and prognosis, changing the subject when it arose. As Hinton commented, 'Undoubtedly, like adults, not all children necessarily want to consider explicitly the likelihood of dying.'[6]

However, other children welcome the opportunity to discuss their futures or have their questions answered and will raise the topic with those they feel are able and willing to answer or listen. Sometimes parents and children talk to each other about the coming death, saying goodbye and expressing love and gratitude for all they have shared; such exchanges leave precious memories.[7]

Unfortunately, the changing image of death, which has accompanied the raising of standards by the hospice movement, can result in unreal expectations: 'Often it seems as if one caricature has replaced another. The old image of death, negative and despairing, the new positive but "rose-tinted".'[8]

The impending death may be too painful a subject to be broached between the child and parents: what is coming is their separation and for both the sadness is intense. Often neither can face causing or seeing yet more pain in the other. Recognising this, and seeking to protect their parents, children often look to others who, however involved, are at a greater emotional distance and therefore may be confided in or questioned with less danger of unendurable emotions being stirred. Whoever is confided in 'should listen to what the children say, taking cues from them, answering only what they ask and on their terms'.[9]

Some children may find no one willing or able to share their concerns. As Hinton wrote: 'Very few people feel adequate to frank conversation with a dying child.'[10] These children may suffer from feelings of isolation and loneliness. However, Bluebond-Langner stressed that children fear and dislike physical isolation far more than psychological isolation: they want their parents to be with them more than they want to share with them their thoughts and fears.[11]

Talking about death

In the difficult days before the children died, the parents interviewed worried about how much to tell their child. They were torn between wanting to protect the child from a (to them) terrible knowledge and wanting to be quite honest.

Several of the parents were advised to be honest with their children and to give them opportunities to talk about their condition. Some recalled how much they had dreaded the possibility of having to tell their children they were dying. They had accompanied their children through so many terrible events, had had to give them so much bad news, and been unable to save them from suffering. The prospect of having to confirm to them that they would die, and cope with their reactions (along with their own grief), was hard to bear.

Parents of children of all ages commented that the older the child, the more difficult the question of what and how to tell them about their future. Parents of very young children said they were glad that at least they did not have to cope with difficult questions.

In fact, none of the parents mentioned having to answer a direct question about death, although many of the children asked 'Will I ever get better?' Nor did any parents recall informing their child that he or she would die, although several recalled that such questions were put to outsiders. Many of the children indicated to their parents and others, directly or symbolically, that they knew what was happening, on occasion settling anxieties about what and how to tell them about their future.

A mother described her daughter's dawning awareness: 'She didn't realise she was dying until I suppose six or seven weeks beforehand. She just knew, it fell into place what was happening. We never told her out straight "You're going to die, the doctors weren't able to cure you". They wanted to tell her she had another tumour on her spine but we wouldn't let them. From little things she'd say you'd know she was aware of what was happening. She said to me once, "Will I be in a wheelchair for the rest of my life?" At this stage it hadn't registered with her that she wasn't going to get better. This was how I got to know that she was aware of what was happening. She woke up in the middle of the night and she asked me to turn on the light and she said she was afraid to go to sleep in case she didn't wake up. I said "Oh, you'll waken up and I'll be here when you wake up." She said "Just in case I don't, Ma, I love you and I love Daddy and I love John and Paul [her brothers]." Oh, once she said that, I said to myself "She knows what's happening now". I think there were times when she woke up she was surprised she was still here. "Will I see you again, Ma?" she'd say [her mother's voice broke as she remembered this], "Will I see you again, Ma?" '

Another twelve-year-old girl questioned a neighbour and a hospital doctor about her condition: her little sister had told her the children in school were saying she was dying. Both reassured her, saying in effect that she would live for some time yet. One day she asked her father: 'Why are you and Mammy so good to me? Is it because I'm going to die?' Her father replied that it was because she was so sick, ' "because we love you and we're sorry that you're not running round like the other children." Then the two arms went round my neck and she told she loved me and it was perfect.' Another day, after being out in the hospice garden, 'She put her hand back on my hand on the wheelchair and said "Thanks, Da", and she was saying "Thanks for everything", and at the back of it all she was saying "It's not your fault". I'd say she knew all along she was dying but she could protect you, she wouldn't put you through something if she could spare you, and she did, there's no doubt about that.'

The mother of a seven-year-old said she felt it was very important 'to let your child know you know how he feels and that you are upset he's so ill. All the time I would have kept the brave face on, I would never have cried... [but one day] he was so ill and he had terrible pain in his ear and he was in a terrible state. I cried my heart out in front of him, I said "I'm crying because you're so unwell and there's so little I can do for you". Then he started comforting me and there was such a relief in him, it was as if a weight had gone from him; I suppose it was because for the first time he was sharing his anxiety about his own illness.'

A nine-year-old boy worked out for himself what disease he had. His mother recalled: 'It was a while before we were able to talk about it; at first we just told him it was a blood disorder, but I think he was a lot more intelligent than we gave him credit for. He had it all worked out what unit he was in.' Asked why he had not mentioned before that he knew he had leukaemia, the boy responded with logic: 'If I knew and you knew, there wasn't much point in one of us saying it to the other, was there?' Pressed on the point he said, 'If it's something bad I don't want to know about it', and his mother then 'explained to him that it was pretty bad but that the results of treatment were promising, some people had remissions for years and years, and he accepted it. Really, he was very logical about the whole thing all the way through.'

This boy used to 'come out with all sorts of statements and always when he was playing or doing something else. We never discussed [dying] with him but he'd catch you unawares, he'd think he was going to trap you into an answer. Just before his second relapse he asked me "What's going to happen if I go out of remission again?" I said "I don't know. What do you think will happen?" He just looked at me and said "I won't be around any longer." He knew all along, he was quite intelligent, he had it all worked out in his own mind, he knew several little ones had died above [in the hospital]. You couldn't fool him, you couldn't hide anything from him.'

A few weeks before he died, at the age of eleven, this boy remarked that 'he felt like an old man of eighty' and went on to say: 'Some people have a long number of years and others don't.' His mother said he was trying to prepare his parents, 'trying to make it easier for us. I can see an awful lot of what he said was geared towards preparing us.'

A mother remembered her seven-year-old asking 'Will I ever get better?' 'The doctor always told us to tell her the truth, to be straight with her [but] the occasion never arose that she asked us out straight [was she going to die]. I'd say she knew more than we did.' Her husband added: 'Either she didn't know, or she knew and she didn't care, she never indicated that she was worried about the future or anything...she just sort of carried on and deteriorated, rapidly in the finish. She never indicated what she thought, I certainly never asked her, I felt that at her age we couldn't tell her, that would be wrong — we were under worry and strain enough, she wouldn't have to go through it anyway.' This child's mother was certain that the doctor had told her she would not recover. 'He told her to tell Mammy [what he had said] but she wouldn't.'

Three other children, however, were very upset by information given to them by doctors. A GP spoke to an eight-year-old when his mother was out of the room: 'He got into a terrible state that day after she left, he cried and asked me what did the doctor know. I think she let him know that he wasn't going to get well, she was talking to him about going back to hospital. I never saw him so upset.'

A fourteen-year-old girl was greatly distressed to be told in hospital, with neither of her parents present, that unless she had a transplant she had only a year to live.

A fifteen-year-old boy, on a visit to the United States to see a specialist, was told in his parents' presence that spots on X-rays of his lungs were cancerous tumours. 'It nearly killed him;

Last days

he cried, he wouldn't talk to us, he lost interest in everything.'

An eight-year-old's mother wondered whether they should have discussed his illness with him more, but his father felt he was too young: 'If he asked me [would he get better] I would say "I'm praying for you to get well".... There were times during his illness he knew, when he'd get the pain badly he'd say to me "Daddy, it'll do something to me" — he meant it was going to kill him.' The child's mother said, discussing his last days: 'He knew in the end, naturally enough. The morning he died he said "I want to die, there's nothing for me, lying over there." I said "You're a good boy, God wants you." '

One father was troubled by the lack of discussion with his six-year-old son. He and his wife had been advised to give the child opportunities to talk about his illness. Referring to the literature on the benefits of an 'open' approach to communication with the dying, he said: 'The argument seems to be that when a person is dying and can discuss their impending death there can be this enormously rewarding experience and exchange.' This father was torn between regret that there had been no discussion, and concern that he had not adopted a totally positive approach, assuring the child he would recover. His wife, however, pointed out that the child himself had set the pace: he had been anxious to go back to school, 'hounded me to get the books and the uniform, and suddenly there was no more talk of school'. One evening the child woke up suddenly and asked his father 'Am I dead yet?' His father replied 'Why! Do you think you are in heaven?', and then felt he had fluffed the opportunity to talk to his son about his approaching death. But his wife said: 'If he had wanted to talk he would have come back to it. You can't force it.' However, the child's father was not convinced and continued to express his regrets.

Another couple were concerned because they had not told their ten-year-old son that he was dying: 'It was the one thing that worried us. We didn't actually tell him he had secondaries, the reason was to keep his hope alive. But he knew, and we knew he did, that he was deteriorating. He was too intelligent not to know he was weakening. He used to ask "Will I get better?" and our answer was "We're praying night and day that you will." But we hadn't told him his chances were slim. I know it's absurd but I had this image of him reaching heaven and saying "They never told me!" That bothered us. We didn't know what to do. We weren't in a position to say "You're going to die"; the Lord is the only one to decide when and where....' A few nights before he died, the boy raised the question of death, saying people could die anytime, he himself could die tomorrow. His parents asked him 'Are you afraid to die?', he said 'no, God will mind me'. The child's response set his parents' minds at rest: 'That answered everything.'

The mother of another eleven-year-old said: 'He never mentioned death. Near the end I was trying to talk to him about God, he must have guessed a little. I never really asked him was he afraid.... I wouldn't because I'd have to cope with his answer.'

Another mother said of her five-year-old son: 'I had a fear of him knowing. He didn't indicate he knew he was terribly ill, or else we weren't receptive to it.... Maybe we hadn't faced the reality of him knowing.'

A fourteen-year-old boy, bed-ridden with a brain tumour for many months, would 'try to sound out a person, what you'd think, you'd always have to be alert. It was very hard to talk about the future. If I was on my own especially he'd say "Would you think I'll ever get better?" ' This mother, like others, retained hope that her child would be saved and wanted to keep up her son's morale. She said: 'I'd gone to the stage of persuading him [he would recover] and I nearly believed it myself. I didn't want him to know because I was afraid he would give up. At the back of my mind I knew he was going to die but at the same time I felt surely in this length of time something will turn up, there could be something.' This boy, like some others, questioned and confided in outsiders. He told a visitor: 'They all come to me for prayers and they're all getting better bar myself.' As his mother said: 'He wouldn't say it to us but he would say it to someone else. We'd realise [then] what he was thinking.' The boy had said he liked and trusted one of the hospital doctors because 'he was straight with me. He said if the treatment didn't work I would die.'

One day this boy questioned the GP in his mother's presence: 'Will I get my eyesight back, will I get my hearing — it's inclined to go?' When the doctor tried to reassure him, the boy leapt out of bed, seized the doctor round the neck and implored him: 'You must do something for me. Just tell me out straight: am I going to die?' The boy's mother 'ran out of the room, it really affected me, that was the worst, those parts'. This boy 'always wanted someone in the room, all the time; if you left the room, you might sneak out for something, he'd miss you, he'd call you to say that he wanted something just to let you see that he'd missed you.'

Last hours
During their last hours, a number of children indicated, either by symbolic actions or changes in behaviour, that they were aware that their lives were coming to an end.

A seven-year-old girl, who was admitted to hospital a few days before she died 'was beginning to get uneasy. She was fixing everything on the bed, and she said "I want everything put away and tidy"; she wanted the television out, and everything had to be in its place, and she left sweets aside for the doctor. She was tired, she said. But no matter what way she lay she was uncomfortable.'

On the day an eight-year-old boy died, his father watched as 'he sat up and opened his eyes. I never saw him as bright in the eyes'. The child took a toy, a little plastic man, and put him inside a toy van: 'He shut him up, and he smiled and turned on his side. The pain must have all gone for he hadn't lain on his side for four months.' Later the child told his mother he wanted to die.

A mother related of her eleven-year-old son: 'He fitted just about everything into the few hours before he died. It was like he was preparing to go somewhere. Everything had to be arranged the way he wanted it. He brushed his teeth, did the dental floss meticulously through each tooth...his hands were so weak, he dropped the dental floss and I picked it up and put it into the little holder. He sort of dozed for a few minutes and then he said "Where's my dental floss?" and I said "I put it back". "Show it to me", he said, and I had to get it out of the locker and show it. He wanted his new runners taken out and put under the bed. His foot had never grown in almost two years, he'd been a size three, but about two weeks before we had got the new runners in Dunnes and they were a size four and he had been thrilled to bits. "I'm a size four, I'm growing." ' So the new runners were put under the bed. 'He told a joke. Then he wanted me to say a prayer, he was too tired to say it himself. I said the Hail Mary for him, and I said "Do you want me to say any more?", and he said "No, that's fine now." He fixed his [religious] medals both sides of his shoulders and his scapulars and his rosary beads at the other side.'

The night before he died a teenage boy became very talkative and for the only time during his illness asked for an injection.

Most of the children died peacefully; one died in pain, and another fought for breath until about ten minutes before death. Three had seizures or other frightening episodes in the hours before death.

A day or so before he died a teenage boy 'started to get very agitated. It was the first time in a few weeks that he turned round in the bed on his own...and then he started vomiting blood.' This boy, whose symptoms were exceptionally difficult, suffered to the end, in spite of all the devoted efforts of his parents, GP and public health nurse.

A two-year-old was in a coma for several weeks before she died. Her parents took it in turns to watch over her at night. Her mother said that, for her, her daughter died when she lost consciousness. It was suggested to these parents that they try to drip water into the child's mouth 'to keep her alive longer', but as far as they were concerned this was merely prolonging her suffering.

Last days

Three children whose pain was well controlled died peacefully at home: A ten-year-old 'had such happiness. He was emaciated but one day he said "I don't know why I'm so happy today." He wasn't in any pain, he just wasted away, and he never lost control of any of his functions...he had a lovely death.'

A six-year-old had been lying in a foetal position, then sat up suddenly and complained about his eyes. Then 'he was lying back on the pillows and he threw his arms around his Mammy...we just held him...his passage was easy.'

A twelve-year-old girl was conscious until she died. Her mother recalled: 'She wanted me to get into the bed with her and I did.' Visitors came but 'she wasn't in form for them at all'. They left. 'She said "Lie down" and then she said "I can't see the television." After a few minutes she said "Lie in near to me". [She started to make a sound] Her two eyes were in a complete stare. So I knew she was going then and I said it to her. I said "You're going to heaven now" [she made a sign with her finger] and it was like as if she wanted to say something but there was nothing coming out.'

'So then we were talking to her for a good while, telling her one day Mammy and Daddy would come to heaven too. We tried to make it as nice as we could, I suppose.... Just before she drew her last breath — she'd been completely still for about two and a half hours — she turned her head over to me and she turned back to her Daddy, she drew her last breath and that was it. It was like as if we were on her mind right up to the end, she had thought of us right up to the very end.'

CHAPTER 11

Grief

'You know there's no such thing as a last day — there's only a new beginning.'

In the days immediately following their child's death, parents often felt calm and relieved that their child was no longer suffering.

A mother said: 'Throughout that time we weren't really that upset at the death. It probably sounds an awful thing to say; we cried after a time, but I in particular had cried an awful lot throughout the illness and I didn't have many tears left by the time it came. There's a shock that comes with it too. We both sobbed our hearts out about an hour after he died and then we pulled ourselves together.' 'We're not saying we wanted her to die but we'd sooner she passed on then because her tummy got enormous, enormous like a pregnant woman. At the latter end she used to sit up on a chair.'

A father recalled: 'It got to the stage where — God forgive us for saying it — we were asking "When is it going to happen?"'

The parents of a little girl who was in a coma at home for three weeks before she died took it in turns to look after her at night. Her mother said she was disappointed one morning when she woke up and realised that since her husband hadn't woken her the child was still alive.

The parents of a teenager said that when he died 'We were so relieved that he was out of suffering.'

A father felt peaceful after his nine-year-old daughter died: 'I wasn't glad that she was gone but I was glad that all her suffering was over. There was no more of her crying over her stomach...a lot of weight lifted off my shoulders. I just felt, at least I know she's happy now. She died smiling.'

A mother said of her seven-year-old: 'When she died it was sort of a relief, everything happened for me four months before she died.'

Grief

A few parents remarked on the way in which their calm contrasted with the reactions of others and left them feeling that roles had been turned upside-down.

A two-year-old boy died very peacefully at home in his father's arms. The family doctor called to confirm the death, and when he saw the child laid out in the cot he burst into tears. The mother, six months pregnant, helped him down the stairs: 'I was fairly calm and I was trying to be calm and matter of fact about it and deal with everybody, and I was annoyed with him for getting upset and upsetting me.'

A father said when his twelve-year-old daughter died: 'We weren't devastated immediately, there was such peace. We were quite calm. There must be some mechanism in the brain that shuts it off. The priest and nurses were crying but we weren't. I worried about that. There was a young girl, a friend of my daughter's, roaring crying and I ended up consoling her. The roles were all higgledy-piggledy.' This father remarked wryly that when a neighbour's child had been killed, one of her other children had said to her: 'You must have loved Mary an awful lot because you never cry so much for us.' After his own child died his son said to a neighbour: 'Mam and Dad don't seem very upset.' As the father said: 'We kept up for the children's sake but it seems you can't win.'

One couple were asked to do an interview about their son for a local newspaper. They refused initially but their local priest persuaded them to change their minds, saying to them: 'Other people have needs too.' These and other parents commented on the shock of the death: 'By the time she did die I was fairly well prepared for it, in the sense that we knew [she was going to die], but I suppose you're never really prepared for it. It was still a shock when she died.'

A father said: 'You still get the bang when it happens, nothing ever prepares you for that.' And a mother recalled: 'It's afterwards that it really hits you.'

Most of the children who died at home were laid out there, and 'waked' for a few days before the funeral Mass and burial. 'We waked her at home for two days. This was very good for

Children's Last Days

the other children. They knew exactly what had happened — she wasn't sick one moment and gone the next.' 'He died on Sunday. We knew where he was going to be waked, we had a room prepared, there was no question of him being removed to anywhere.'

In a few cases the mothers laid out their children themselves, but generally other relatives, nurses or parish sisters did so. One mother said: 'I did it and I didn't mind doing it at all. I was very glad I had done it. I would probably recommend to other people to do it if they were able to do it.' Another mother had wanted to lay out her little daughter: 'I had it all built up that if I could I would lay out the child, that if I couldn't do that much for her...', but others took over. A father complained that the coffin provided for his little son was too big: 'When we put him into the coffin he was lost in it — it was too deep.... They had this pad that your head rests on, it was too big, it was for an adult....'

The community continued to support families: 'It's a tradition in our parish that the local people dig the grave...the funeral, the community took over...they all walked into town behind the hearse, the school had a guard of honour....' Another family was very grateful that neighbours organised the funeral, even directing the traffic round the narrow country roads: 'They organised things we wouldn't think of, you just don't think, you're not able to think, for somebody to take over something like that, you really do appreciate it.' Families remembered with pride the packed churches, the flower-laden graves. But when it was all over they had to live with the loss of their child.

Many of the parents said the pain of loss had been far greater than they had expected. The fact that they had known the child was dying did not seem to lessen their grief: 'You're never prepared for it really, never. Even though you anticipate it and you know in your heart and soul that this is what's going to happen, when it happens it's a different thing, isn't it?' 'Nothing prepares you for the loss of a child. I had lost my parents, but a child....' 'We thought we had suffered, we

thought we knew all about pain when he was lying there for six weeks...no one could tell you what the pain of loss is like.'
'The one thing that really shocked us, we thought we were sort of prepared...the pain [of grief] was dreadful and there was nothing and no way...before that I had no idea it could be so bad.'

Living with bereavement

Parents do not 'get over' the death of their child: 'It is often observed that grieving for a lost child never entirely ends.'[1] Bereaved parents often have different reactions from those experienced after other deaths. Their grief frequently becomes more rather than less intense with time, and the second and sometimes third year after loss may be even worse than the first.[2] Although the intensity of mourning eventually diminishes with time — if it did not, it would be impossible to go on living — bereaved parents have continually to work at accepting and living with the loss.[3]

Most of the parents I interviewed were very recently bereaved: one couple had lost their child only a few months before our meeting; the longest interval between a death and my interview with parents was two years nine months. Some of the parents said they were finding their loss more difficult to bear as time passed. 'They say that time eases all pain but I think it's more that as time goes on the more it hurts...there's an awful hole in there inside.' A father said he found his grief harder to bear as time went on. A mother said her pain was 'worse now than in the beginning'.

A father said: 'It's an awful burden. It's very hard to accept it. [The pain] is easing if you're busy, it goes off your mind, but it comes back. There's no day in the two years that he didn't come into my mind, I don't put him out of my mind either. How do you forget people anyway? My own mother died thirty years ago — I never forget her. They're two people that are on my mind all the time.'

Grief was evoked in terms of emptiness and physical pain. A father talked of 'that terrible ache, that inward suffering and the longing that's in you, and it's further in you and you just have to stop thinking because you could go to rack yourself, thinking.' 'The heartache is always with us, he's always in our thoughts.' 'There's nothing worse than parting with a child, you know that.' 'The absence and total loss is dreadful. While she was here there was always a chance of a miracle or something, but death robs us of that. Death is so final.' 'The loss is terrible when they're gone, it's a terrible feeling.' 'The sadness, all that might have been, there are times that ache in your heart is there. No matter what, the circle is broken, he is gone....'

Some parents discussed how they coped with their sorrow, and about other people's reactions. A mother said she found it hard to meet visitors: 'The first few weeks after he was gone I felt I just wanted to get into myself and be left alone to grieve alone. I just couldn't meet the people and talk to them. My husband could, no matter who came.' Her husband said: 'You have to eventually stop talking about them to the public because after a week or two it's your problem. It's inwardly there, there's a hole in there that'll never be filled, and that's yours.'

A father had resisted attempts to make him talk about his loss: 'My grief will be my own and I'll do it my way.' A husband and wife had similar attitudes. Their young son had died two years and some months before the interview. The child's mother said: 'I don't know can anyone understand. They don't understand what you're going through unless they've been through it.... I never found that people were unsympathetic, or hard-hearted, or tried to avoid me or anything like that. I think it's how you cope with it yourself, that other people react to you. If you're taking it very hard or getting upset all the time, not able to talk about it, people will shy away from you because they won't know how to cope with it, but if you're coping to a certain extent and you're able to talk about it...you will break down from time to time but you can't be all the time moping.'

Her husband agreed: 'If you feel bad all the time, you pitify

Grief

yourself, you're doing it for yourself, you're sorry for yourself.' His wife continued: 'I try to tell myself that's what we're all striving for. If you believe it, if you're a Christian and you believe in these things, the child's an angel. We've to go through life, we've to work for it and we've to suffer for it, if you like, where he got the easy way, really. People say to me "He's a little angel, he's better off", so it's just yourself you're feeling for. You could be forever asking yourself questions and wondering why this and why that, and there's no answer — nobody has the answer. You blame yourself...you wonder could it have been your fault, did you neglect something, was there anything you could have done different, all sorts of emotions, feelings.'

Another mother said: 'It wasn't easy to go on, I think you wonder how you're going to live without him [the dead child]. Before he died I used to say how are we going to live, how are we going to cope. It's funny, life just goes on, it just keeps moving even though you want it to stop, one day follows the next...which is a good thing, if everything stayed black just because you wanted it to....'

Two couples mentioned that they found consolation in the thought that their child would always be with them, unlike their other children: 'No matter how old we get we'll still have a little boy of eight. He's never going to grow up and get old.... In a way when the others have left us he will always be with us.' 'The void will always be there till the end of time, but I think of how he coped with it and his courage and I have to get out of it.'

Some parents struggled with feelings of disbelief: 'It's so hard to grasp, even at this stage, so hard.' The mother of a child who died when she was twelve years old said: 'It's hard to believe it sometimes, to think of her going around with all the girls, and they're still going around doing what they used to.' A father recalled that in the months following his son's death: 'There was for me almost total disbelief — it hasn't happened, he's still there, because he's so real still, he's still there, the grin....' A mother said of her son's illness: 'It was a strange time, because when I look back, some of it just doesn't seem real. Sometimes I wonder if it happened at all. I look over his photographs just to remind me he really was there....'

The 'special child'
Many of the parents spoke of their pride in their sick child, the courage and maturity developed over the course of the illness, and the special relationship that grew up between them: 'For the time she was ill it made her grow up very fast. They have to come to terms with life very quickly, very early, far too early. She never caused us the slightest bit of trouble. She was lovely, she really was.' 'He lived every minute of his life to the full.' 'He was a character really. Full of wit and wisdom not taught to him by anybody, just there.' 'He was so special...he was fantastic until he got ill...they're not for this world. He was a great, great child.' 'These children are something else. Any of them I've come into contact with, they're different really, any of them.' 'I do sometimes think they're unique — or is it their illness makes them that way?' 'She never gave us any trouble, she was an easy patient.' 'She came on a lot in the last six months — she packed a lot into her two years, a life-time.' 'Your whole life is centred round the youngest child, our lives were, he was with us everywhere.' 'She was marvellous really — that made it easier on us.' 'He enjoyed life, every minute he was good he enjoyed it.' 'He made it so easy for us. He had an extremely positive outlook on life.'

'When I was reading some little prayer with him, the Last Day came into it. He said "You know there's no such thing as a last day — there's only a new beginning." From a six-year-old child — where does it come from? You really knew that he knew a hell of a lot more than you did.'

'We found that he matured so much throughout his illness and all the trauma that he was quite a different boy at the end of the nine months, that he had matured. He was a marvellous boy, he really was, and we have these wonderful memories.

Grief

He was a gift. He had a lovely life, he had a lovely death. He was just three weeks short of his tenth birthday when he died, but really he had achieved more in that time than some who live to be ninety.' A few days before he died this boy said to his parents: 'I love talking to you like this.' 'He was telling us how great we were, he was a very affectionate and loving child.'

The sick children became special both in themselves and in their relations to others. Their threatened futures made them doubly precious to their parents. The intensity of love and care, the mutual protection and concern, the heightened sensitivity, all made the parents' relationships with these children out of the ordinary. Parents were faced with what had been unthinkable and struggled to absorb it. At times it seemed their children were ahead of them in understanding what was happening; perhaps their failing bodies signalled to them that life was ebbing.

Because of all they had to endure the children were forced to confront the reality of sickness and death. They had had to submit to invasive and often painful treatment, to adapt to the strange world of hospital, to cope with baldness, obesity, the loss of a limb, the narrowing of their lives. Such trials called on their resources of courage, adaptability and acceptance, and on their anger too, the adolescents' desire to live expressed in the rage of frustration. They developed in maturity so that they became wise beyond their years, coming to understand in a few months what others may not discover in a long lifetime. They sought and sometimes found their own answers to the great existential questions 'Why?' and 'Why me?'.

At the end of it all some parents found themselves so drained and preoccupied with their grief for the lost child that they stopped feeling for other members of the family. One husband said to his wife: 'For months you felt nothing for anybody in this house.' She agreed: 'It must be very hard on the other children because I'm only beginning to love them now, again, only beginning. I stopped loving them, really, the day he died.... I would do the same for any of them, I wouldn't hesitate. I'd run out and give my life for them in the morning, but I stopped *feeling* love for them. For a long time, he's dead about seven months now, it was all surface love...even though I was hugging them and holding them...it's like as if they're out there, as if I'm in a little island and there's the sea all around and they're out there and I'm distant from them.'

A father, tortured with grief, said that though he loved his other children, 'If God took them all away and gave me back my darling even for one hour it'd be worth it.' The mother who found herself gazing at photographs to reassure herself that her son had once existed said: 'I miss him something desperate.... I sit and mull over it and go back over it.... I thought at first that being the eldest that was why we loved him so much. Then when he died I didn't feel that I loved them [the other children] at all, and even now sometimes I can't feel anything for them. I think he took a lot of my love.... Before he was sick that wasn't the way, I knew that I loved them all, but when he died...nothing meant anything really. Even still at times nothing really means anything. Yet I've still got other kids, life is still full or should be.... I've never said that to anyone that I loved him a lot more, but I think that's the truth of it.'

A number of parents talked about their attitude to life and death, saying that their values had changed, they now had a different perspective. A young mother said: 'I think life must be very very short.' She, like some other parents, said she would have welcomed death for herself: 'If someone told me I was dying it wouldn't worry me that much. The one thing that would worry me would be leaving the family, but as regards myself I wouldn't worry. I'm sorry I'm not older — because I've to live so much longer. I'd prefer to be sixty. I think it would be much easier on me, because I've a lot of life to live yet. People talk about going back to work, I don't really want to. If I was sixty it would be easier just to sit back.' A husband and wife both agreed: 'It wouldn't cost a thought to go. We'd have him there.' Asked had his son's death changed his attitude to death, a father replied: 'It has changed my attitude to life. There are no problems any more: problems that people call problems, I don't call them problems any more, you don't tend to panic over them, don't bother getting worked up over them. A sick child — that's what I call a problem.' A mother said the same thing: 'Other problems pale into insignificance compared to what you've coped with.'

In caring for the sick child and the family, in maintaining some kind of normal life, in keeping their nerve in the face of repeated crises, parents had to call on all their resources. In overcoming fear and fatigue, day after day and night after night, controlling their grief because their child needed them to be calm, they faced a trial like no other.

As one father said: 'None of us would have chosen that our child would die, but there was something honourable about it, there was a certain pride at the end of it. We did what we could and we did it to the best of our ability and we have no regrets. We are sad and we'll always have the sadness, but we'll also have our pride.' His wife added: 'He's safe now, it was a privilege, we looked after him from the cradle to the grave. Death isn't the most terrible thing that can happen to anyone. If you have loved, and experienced love, you have everything.'

APPENDIX

Details of sample and method

The twenty couples I interviewed constituted a convenience sample of parents of children who had died, mainly of cancer. Of the twenty children and adolescents concerned, nineteen had died from various forms of cancer and one from a disorder similar to cystic fibrosis.

Identifying and contacting parents

1 Population

The population from which the main sample was drawn consisted of the parents of children aged one to fourteen years who had died of cancer, other than unexpectedly, during a twenty-one month period (seven quarters) in the late 1980s. A total of seventy-six deaths from cancer of children in this age-group was recorded for the period, although it is possible that this figure is an underestimate of the actual numbers of deaths. Some childhood cancer deaths may be recorded as being due to more proximate causes such as pneumonia or heart failure. (Central Statistics Office, various years, Department of Health, 1986, p 22.) An unknown number of children, but at least four, died suddenly from complications of disease or treatment. (Breatnach 1990.) Thus the population of main interest numbered about seventy families.

The majority of the children concerned were treated in the oncology unit of Our Lady's Hospital for Sick Children in Crumlin which, at the time of the study, treated about seventy per cent of children in Ireland who develop cancer. The unit had a case load at any one time of approximately four hundred children, and about seventy new cases per annum.

About thirty per cent of children with cancer were treated

Appendix

in other hospitals which had attending oncology consultants. In some cases care is shared between consultants in Dublin hospitals and consultants in hospitals nearer to the families' homes. A small but unknown number of children and adolescents with brain tumours are seen by neurologists and/or surgeons and are not treated by cancer specialists.

2 Sample
I identified and contacted the parents of thirty-one children and adolescents (two from one family) in four ways:

(a) with the co-operation of the oncology unit in Our Lady's Hospital for Sick Children, Crumlin;
(b) with the co-operation of consultants from other hospitals, hospice doctors, GPs and hospice nurse;
(c) with the co-operation of participating parents;
(d) other.

a) Crumlin
The selection of potential interviewees was made by hospital staff, the main criteria being that the child's death had been expected, had taken place about six months previously, and the child was aged between one and fourteen years. Parents who were thought by the hospital staff not to be ready to be interviewed or who were known to be undergoing additional stresses were not approached.

During the period of study about forty-five of the children treated in Crumlin died, four of them unexpectedly. Three families went to live abroad after the child's death and were not available for interview.

Interviews took place over a two-year period in four phases, at roughly six-monthly intervals. This schedule, and the uneven pattern of deaths, influenced the selection of parents for participation in the study. Twenty couples were contacted, in four phases, by the consultant who wrote a covering letter to my invitations to participate in the study. Forms and stamped addressed envelopes for replies were enclosed.

Fifteen couples eventually agreed to take part, one couple refused, three couples and a single parent did not reply. Two couples were not interviewed for practical reasons; another couple was not included because when I contacted them I found that one of the parents was too distressed to participate at that time.

(b) Other consultants, hospice staff, GPs
I contacted ten consultants and hospice doctors and one hospice nurse who care for children with cancer, asking for their help in identifying and contacting parents to take part in the study. Three did not reply, seven agreed to help, and one refused.

In the event, one of the consultants identified the families of two children, and I wrote to them. The consultant noted that one of the couples he identified had been 'annoyed' with him because they felt he was a bit slow in diagnosing the problem. His openness in facilitating contact with this family is admirable. The parents in question did not respond. The parents of the second child agreed to participate and I interviewed them. Two hospice doctors each identified one couple; both couples agreed to take part. A hospice nurse and a GP each identified one couple; both couples agreed to participate.

One of the children in this group had been treated in Crumlin. The child's parents agreed to participate and I interviewed them. This couple was included in Crumlin's list of potential interviewees. Thus twenty of the forty potential interviewee couples from Crumlin were invited to take part, and thirteen did so. Thirteen (sixty-six per cent) of the nineteen children with cancer included in the study had been treated in the Crumlin oncology unit.

(c) Participating parents
One mother contacted me directly having heard about the research from a GP and I interviewed her and her husband. One of the participating mothers identified three more couples;

Appendix

two refused to take part, one agreed to take part and I interviewed them.

(d) Other
I contacted the parents of a child who died from a disease similar to cystic fibrosis via RTE which had broadcast an interview with the girl's father. The girl's parents were deeply dissatisfied with the circumstances surrounding their daughter's death.

TABLE 1

Identification and contact of parents

	Contacts	Yes	No	No resp.	Outcome Interviews
Crumlin	20	15	1	4	12*
Other doctors and nurse	6	5		1	5
Participating parents	4	2	2		2
Other	1	1			1
Total	31	23	3	5	20

*Three of the Crumlin contacts who responded positively were not interviewed, for practical reasons in two cases, and because one of the parents was too distressed in the third case.

There were six girls and thirteen boys in the cancer sample, reflecting the increased vulnerability of boys to malignant disease. Five of the children had leukaemia, four had neuroblastomas, four had osteosarcomas, two had brain tumours, and the remaining four had tumours of the liver, adrenal gland, kidney, and spine. One of the children with leukaemia also had Down's Syndrome. The remaining child suffered from a non-malignant disease akin to cystic fibrosis.

TABLE 2

Children's diagnoses

Cancers:

leukaemia	5
neuroblastoma	4
osteosarcoma	4
brain tumours	2 (3)*
other tumours	4
Other disease:	1
Total	20

*one child developed a fatal brain tumour after being treated for three years for leukaemia.

The age range of the children in the sample was from two to fifteen years, the mean was 8.4 years.

TABLE 3

Children's ages (at death)

ages of children	*number of children*
2–4 years	4
5–9 years	9
10–15 years	7
Total no of children	20

Most (12 out of 20) of the families lived in rural areas; eight of these lived some miles from the nearest village, while four lived in rural villages or small towns. Three families lived in cities or towns, five lived on the outskirts or in the suburbs of towns or cities.

Appendix

TABLE 4

Family homes

urban	1
suburban city	3
suburban town	4
rural town/village	3
rural	9
Total no. of homes	20

Family size, including the child who died, ranged from one to eight, with a mean family size of four children. Four of the mothers were pregnant at the time of the sick child's death.

TABLE 5

Family size, including child who died

number of children	*number of families*
1–2	4
3–4	10
5 or more	6
Total no of families	20

One little girl was the only child of young parents, four children were the first in families of two or more, seven were middle children in families of three or more, and eight were the youngest children in families of two or more.

All of the families were Catholic.

Five of the fathers were in professional/managerial positions, two were small farmers, four worked as non-managerial employees in the state sector, four were skilled industrial workers, and five had their own businesses, ranging in size from a small shop to a factory employing over twenty people.

The majority (fifteen) of the mothers worked mainly in the

home, although some assisted informally in family businesses; five had full-time employment, but all gave up their jobs in the course of the child's illness. Three of the fathers gave up their jobs to help in caring for the family during the child's illness.

TABLE 6: Parents' occupations

Mother:		Father:	
full time at home*	15	professional/managerial	5
teacher	3	own business: more than five employees	2
other professional	2	own business: 1–5 employees including family	3
		skilled industrial worker	4
		non-managerial, white collar	4
		small farmer	2
Total	20	Total	20

*Three of the mothers assisted informally with the family business.

TABLE 7: Socio-economic group of families*

Group	No of families
1. Higher professional, lower professional, employer or manager	7
2. Salaried employee, intermediate non-manual worker	4
3. Other non-manual worker	2
4. Skilled manual worker	5
6A Farmer, farmer's relative or farm manager, other agricultural worker or fisherman	2
Total number of families	20

*categories as used in 1986 Census of Population (Central Statistics Office)

Appendix

Comparison of sample with population

The absolute numbers concerned, both in the population and in the sample, are so small that detailed statistical analyses or discussions of representativeness are not appropriate. Bias in the selection of interviewees was avoided as far as possible. Some variables such as diagnosis and age of the children with cancer may be compared for the sample and population, but other variables such as the course of the illness, family characteristics, etc are not identifiable or comparable.

TABLE 8

Children (1–14) with cancer: age and diagnostic variables of population and sample*

Age	Pop	Sample	Diagnosis	Pop	Sample
1–4	27	4	leukaemia	25	4
5–14	49	14	other mal.	52	14

* sample total is 18: one of the children was aged fifteen at the time of death so is not included in this table.

All that can be said with certainty is that I identified and contacted the parents of thirty of the approximately seventy children aged one to fourteen years who died (other than suddenly) from cancer during the period of study. I invited them to take part in the study, and eighteen couples did in fact do so. I also interviewed the parents of a boy aged fifteen at the time of his death from cancer, and the parents of a girl who died of a non-malignant long-term disease.

It is likely that the sample under-represents parents who were having particular difficulty coping with their grief. Certain geographical areas are not represented: no family from west of the Shannon is included in the study although I invited three to participate.

The interviews

The aim was to carry out interviews as near to six months after the child's death as was practicable, although I did not achieve this in all cases. Interviews took place from three to twenty-five months after the death, with most (fifteen) taking place after an interval of between five and twelve months.

The six-month interval was chosen on the grounds that the parents would by then have had a chance to absorb the initial shock of the death, to regroup to some extent after the funeral and all the other practical demands, yet the details of the illness would still be vivid. It seemed likely given the experience of Burton (1975, pp 203–4) and others that many parents would welcome the opportunity to talk about their child, and to be of help to other parents in the future. I hoped that at best the interview would be therapeutic and at worst an inconvenience. One of my major concerns was to avoid causing any additional distress to parents: I reassured parents when inviting their participation that they would not be pressed on any topic they did not wish to discuss.

The interviews were tape-recorded and very loosely structured. I simply invited the parents to tell me about their child's terminal illness, beginning with the initial diagnosis of life-threatening disease. In effect it was the parents who set the agenda. By choosing to highlight certain aspects and to downplay others it was they, not I, who set the order of priorities of what they had found important. I had a mental checklist of questions of interest, most of which arose naturally in the course of the interviews. Where they did not it was not always appropriate, given the over-riding requirement of not adding to the parents' distress, to raise them; nor was it always appropriate to pursue or clarify issues.

All of the interviews, except one, took place in the parents' homes at a time convenient to them. In all cases both parents were present for most of the interviews. One interview was held in a private hotelroom at the suggestion of the parents, who were visiting Dublin at the time.

The domestic setting, where the child had lived and in most

cases died, and the joint contribution of parents, were important features of the method which aimed to grasp and understand parents' perspectives. In their homes the parents were in the position of hosts, and indeed were most hospitable. Babies and toddlers were present during some of the interviews, and children of all ages were in and out from time to time during most of the interviews. On one occasion two siblings (aged nine and twelve) were present throughout; because of their presence this interview followed a slightly different course from the others.

Validity
For ethical reasons, and to avoid bias — the aim was to identify parental not professional perceptions — I did not discuss cases, either before or after interviews, with the referring or other professionals.

Given the fallibility of memory, the potential for misunderstanding, and the intensely distressing nature of many of the events recounted, it may be asked how valid are these accounts in objective terms of what actually happened and in terms of subjective feelings and judgements recalled some time after the events. It has been found that although parents may not remember exactly when their child first walked or talked, they do accurately recall their children's serious illnesses and reliably describe and predict how their children behave in a variety of situations. (Chess et al 1966, Thomas et al 1968.) Parents' narrative accounts of their children's behaviour were found to be more reliable sources of data than other methods, such as questionnaire assessments. (Graham et al 1973.)

Thus it may reasonably be assumed that while such details as exact dates, times and so on of events during the terminal illness may not be recalled exactly, the salient features, the landmarks as it were, are accurately reported. In other words, parents in general are valid and reliable witnesses to events concerning their children.

It appears too that parents' memory of their responses is not distorted by any depression or anxiety they may be suffering at the time of the enquiry. Woolley et al (1989) interviewed parents of children with life-threatening illnesses, some of whom had died, about the manner in which they were given the diagnosis, and found no connection between parents' current mental state and their satisfaction or lack of it with the manner in which diagnoses were given.

Notes and references

Note: All works cited below are included in full in the bibliography on page 153.

Chapter 1 Cancer and children
1. Parkin et al 1988, p 1; West 1984
2. CSO 1980s — various years
3. OPCS 1984
4. Mann 1989, p 453
5. Bailey 1979, p 75; Birch 1979, p 3. These figures refer to ethnically similar populations for which reasonably comparable data are available.
6. Department of Health 1986, pp 7-8
7. Birch et al 1980
8. Bailey 1979, p 75; Birch 1979, p 7; Birch et al 1980; Department of Health 1986, pp 12-13; Miller 1988, p 3; Parkin et al 1988, p 1
9. Malpas 1979, pp 12-15; Birch and Marsden 1987; Monson and MacMahon 1984; Gardner et al 1990
10. Morris Jones 1981; West 1984
11. Ward & Oakhill 1988, p 238
12. Kubler Ross 1970; Hinton 1972; Saunders 1978; Lamerton 1980; Saunders et al 1981; Bonica 1985; Zimmerman 1986; Stoddard 1978; Saunders 1981a; Gotay 1983; Mor et al 1988; Dionne 1988
13. Lamerton 1980, p 110; Corr and Corr 1985, Preface; Zimmerman 1986, p 284
14. Buckingham 1983, p 84; Zimmerman 1986, pp 29, 285; Gibbons 1986, p 506; Ward and Oakhill 1988, p 257; Goodall 1988, p 461
15. Tebbi 1987, p vii; Zevon et al 1987, p 346; Papadatou 1989
16. Burton 1974; Chapman and Goodall 1979, 1980; Burne et al 1984, p 1667; OPCS 1985; Eland 1985a, 1985b; Salvage 1986; Thornes 1988
17. Thornes 1988, p 21

Chapter 2 The bombshell
1. Burton 1975, Chapter 3; Gyulay 1978; Maguire et al 1979, p 142; Woolley et al 1989; Lascari 1973, pp 449-53; Waechter 1964, p 16
2. '.... should survive.' Davies 1979, p 151
3. Woolley et al 1989, p 1626. According to an Australian physician the doctor 'should allow himself to show controlled and dignified emotion'. (Ekert 1983.)

Chapter 3 An uncertain future
1. Ekert 1983
2. Donnelly-Wood 1988

Children's Last Days

3   Twycross and Lack 1983, p 321
4   Miser et al 1987
5   Gyulay 1978, p 9; Davies 1979, p 151; Bluebond-Langner 1978, p 216; Miles and Demi 1986, p 111; Schmidt 1987, p 331
6   Ekert 1983
7   For this study I define the terminal period, not in terms of objective clinical factors, but rather as starting when: a) parents were told unequivocally or became aware that their child was going to die and: b) the decision was taken not to persist with or initiate treatment aimed primarily at cure or prolonging life.
8   Morris Jones 1981, p 192
9   Oakhill 1988
10 Ward and Oakhill 1988, p 239; Chambers et al 1989, p 937
10 Donnelly Wood 1988, p 202; Ward and Oakhill 1988, p 241

Chapter 4: Getting information, making decisions
1   Culling 1988, p 223
2   Chapman and Goodall 1980

Chapter 5: Looking for kindness
1   Mott 1990
2   Robertson 1958, 1962; Stacey 1970; Hall and Stacey 1979; Stenbak 1986; McGee and Fitzgerald 1990

Chapter 6: Cancer in the family
1   Culling 1988; Mott 1990; '...whether or not the child will be cured.' Morris Jones 1981, p 192
2   Zevon et al 1987, p 342
3   Gath 1989
4   Burton 1975, pp 191-6, 231-4; Kazak 1989, p 28; Kramer 1984; Gath 1989
5   Rando 1986, pp 30-31
    Author's note: Shortly after our daughter was diagnosed with leukaemia we were told by a member of a parents' support group: 'Of course, you realise that most marriages break up because of the strain of leukaemia.'
6   Karayalcin 1983, p 465; Culling 1988, p 223

Chapter 7: Support from the community
1   Pentol 1982; Lanskey et al 1979; OPCS 1985
2   Bodkin et al 1982
3   Baldwin 1985, p 165; Stein et al 1989, pp 700-1
4   Donnelly Wood 1988
5   Marnham 1980, p 10
6   Marnham 1980, p 9

Notes and references

Chapter 8: Terminal care
1. Similar responses have been noted by Gyulay, 1978 pp 104-5.
2. This issue is discussed by Martin 1985, pp 83-4.
3. Lamerton 1980, p 110; Corr and Corr 1985, Preface; Zimmerman 1986, p 284
4. Saunders quoted in Lamerton 1980, p 108
5. Lewis et al 1987, p 71
6. Lamerton 1980, p 107
7. Waechter 1979; Lascari 1973, p 463; Papadatou 1989; Gyulay 1978, p 16; Wilson 1985; Tebbi 1987, p vii; Zevon et al 1987, p 346
8. Gyulay 1978; Buckingham and Loveday 1983, pp 97-103; Dominica 1985; Ward and Oakhill 1988; Thornes 1988; Harris 1989
9. Dominica 1985; Donnelly-Wood 1988; Ward and Oakhill 1988, p 240
10. Thornes 1988; Wilkes 1986, p 4
11. Martin 1985; Ward and Oakhill, 1988 p 240; Thornes 1988
12. Murray Parkes 1988, p 52
13. Murray 1989

Chapter 9: Pain
1. Saunders 1981b; Baines 1981
2. Vere 1984, p 127
3. Baines 1981; Twycross and Lack 1984
4. Chapman and Goodall 1980; Ward and Oakhill 1988, p 254
5. Lamerton 1980, pp 51-2; Twycross and Lack 1984
6. Twycross and Lack 1984; Walsh 1985
7. Collinge and Stewart 1983, p 149; Chapman and Goodall 1980; Ward and Oakhill 1988
8. Schechter et al 1986
9. Fagerhaugh and Strauss 1977; Saunders 1981b, p 216; Ventafridda and Swerdlow 1984, p 161 Mohide et al 1988
10. Eland 1985b; McGrath and Unruh 1987, p 96
11. Noordenbos, quoted in Prologue to Wall and Melzack 1984
12. Saunders 1981b; Melzack and Wall 1982, Ch 1; McGrath and Unruh 1987, pp 47-53
13. Baines 1981
14. McGrath and Unruh 1987, p 307
15. Eland 1985a; Zeltzer 1989, p 3
16. Foreword to McGrath and Unruh 1987, p xv
17. Zeltzer 1989, p 3; Eland 1985a
18. Haslam 1969; Kaiko 1980; Williamson and Williamson 1983; Gross and Gardner 1980; Schechter et al 1986
19. Barber 1989, p 122; McGrath and Hillier 1989, p 11
20. Chapman and Goodall 1979; Eland 1985b; McGrath and Unruh 1987; Schechter et al 1986

Children's Last Days

21 Eland and Anderson 1977
22 In Foreword to McGrath and Unruh, 1987, p xv
23 McGrath and Unruh 1987, p 235; Zeltzer 1989, p 3; McGrath and Hillier 1989, p 14; Schechter et al 1986; Zeltzer 1989, p 3; McGrath and Hillier 1989, p 7
24 Rana 1987
25 Eland 1985b; Collinge and Stewart 1983, p 149
26 Eland 1985b; McGrath and Unruh 1987
27 Eland 1985b, p 41
28 Katz et al 1980
29 Thornes 1988, p 30
30 Baines 1981; Kohler and Radford 1985; Martinson 1987; Chambers et al 1989

Chapter 10 Last days
1 Gyulay 1978; Bluebond-Langner 1978; Waechter 1972
2 Hinton 1972; Howarth 1979; Lamerton 1980, p 168
3 Twycross and Lack 1983, p 319
4 Waechter 1971, p 107; Hinton 1972, Chapter 10; Bluebond-Langner 1978, p 233; Mott 1982
5 '...most intense fears' Waechter 1971, p 107; '...always divulging truth'. Hinton 1972, p 132; Bluebond-Langner 1978
6 '...and decisions.' Hinton 1972, p 132; '...of dying.' Hinton 1972, p 135
7 Bluebond-Langner 1978; Gyulay 1978, p 151; Buckingham 1983, pp 94-5
8 Twycross and Lack 1983, p 315
9 Bluebond-Langner 1978, p 235
10 Hinton 1972, p 135
11 Bluebond-Langner 1978, p 228

Chapter 11: Grief
1 Osterweis et al 1984, p 83
2 Sanders 1980, Knapp 1986, Rando 1986, Dominica 1987, Delight and Goodall 1988
3 Corr et al 1985, Pine and Brauer 1986

Bibliography

Bailey, C. (1979): 'The management of brain tumours in children' in P.H. Morris Jones (ed) *Topics in Pediatrics 1: Haematology and Oncology*, Tunbridge Wells: Pitman Medical

Baines, M. (1981): 'The principles of symptom control' in C. Saunders, D.H. Summers & N. Teller (eds): *Hospice: the Living Idea*, London: Edward Arnold

Baines, M. (1989): 'Pain relief in active patients with cancer: analgesic drugs are the foundation of management', *British Medical Journal*: 298, 36-8

Baldwin, S. (1985): *The Costs of Caring: Families and Disabled Children*, London: Routledge & Kegan Paul

Barber, J. (1989): 'Suffering children hurt us', *Pediatrician*, Vol 16, Nos 1-2

Betz, C. (1987): 'Death, Dying and Bereavement: a Review of the Literature, 1970-1985' in T. Krulik, B. Holaday & I.M. Martinson (1987) (eds) *The Child and Family Facing Life-Threatening Illness*, Philadelphia: J.B. Lippincott Company

Birch, J.M. (1979): 'The Epidemiology of Childhood Tumours' in Morris Jones, P.H. (ed) *Topics in Pediatrics 1: Haematology and Oncology*, Tunbridge Wells: Pitman Medical

Birch, J.M. & H.B. Marsden (1987): 'A classification scheme for childhood cancer', *International Journal of Cancer*, 40: 620-24

Birch, J.M., H.B. Marsden & R. Swindell (1980): 'Incidence of malignant disease in childhood: a 24-year review of the Manchester Children's Tumour Registry data', *British Journal of Cancer*, 42, 215-23

Bluebond-Langner, M. (1978): *The Private Worlds of Dying Children*, Princeton: Princeton University Press

Bodkin, C.M., T.J. Pigott & J.R. Mann (1982): 'Financial burden of childhood cancer', *British Medical Journal*, Vol 284, 22 May

Bonica, J.J. (1985): 'Treatment of Cancer Pain: Current status and future needs' in H.L. Fields et al (eds), *Advances in Pain Research and Therapy*, vol 9; New York: Raven, pp 589-616

Bowling, A. & A. Cartwright (1982): *Life After a Death*, London: Tavistock Publications

Bozeman, M.F., C.E. Orbach & A.M. Sutherland (1955):'The adaptation of mothers to the threatened loss of their children through leukaemia', *Cancer*, 8: 1–19

Bracken, J.M. (1986): *Children with Cancer: A Comprehensive Reference Guide for Parents*, New York and Oxford: Oxford University Press

Breatnach, F. (1990), personal communication

Buckingham, R. W. (1983): *The Complete Hospice Guide*, New York: Harper & Row

Buckingham, R.W. & L. Loveday (1983): 'Hospice Programs and Dying Children' in R.W. Buckingham *op cit*

Bullimore, J.A. (1979): 'The Diagnosis and Management of Bone Tumours' in P.H. Morris Jones (ed) *Topics in Pediatrics 1: Haematology and Oncology*, Tunbridge Wells: Pitman Medical Publishing

Burne, S.R., F. Dominica & J.D. Baum (1984): 'Helen House — a hospice for children: analysis of the first year', *British Medical Journal*, Vol 289, 15 December, 1665–68

Burton L. (1974): 'Tolerating the Intolerable' in L. Burton (ed) *Care of the Child Facing Death*, London and Boston: Routledge & Kegan Paul

Burton, L. (1975): *The Family Life of Sick Children*, London and Boston: Routledge & Kegan Paul

Byrne, E.A., C.C. Cunningham & P. Sloper (1988): *Families and their Children with Down's Syndrome: One Feature in Common*, London: Routledge & Kegan Paul

Cartwright, A., L. Hockey & J. Anderson (1973): *Life Before Death*, London: Routledge & Kegan Paul

Central Statistics Office (various years): *Vital Statistics*, Dublin: Stationery Office

Central Statistics Office *Census of Population 1986*, Dublin: Stationery Office

Chambers, E.J., A. Oakhill, J.M. Cornish & S. Curnick (1989): 'Terminal care at home for children with cancer', *British Medical Journal*, 298: 937–40

Bibliography

Chambers, T.L. (1987): 'Hospices for Children', *British Medical Journal*, Vol 294, 23 May, 1309–10

LS2 Chapman, J.A. & J. Goodall (1979): 'Dying children need help too', *British Medical Journal*, 1:593–94

Chapman, J.A. & J. Goodall (1980): 'Symptom control in ill and dying children', *Journal of Maternal and Child Health*, 5: 144–54

Chess, S., A. Thomas & H.G. Birch (1966): 'Distortions in developmental reporting made by parents of behaviourally disturbed children', *Journal of American Academic Child Psychiatry*, 5226–34

Collinge, P. & E.D. Stewart (1983): 'Dying Children and Their Families' in J. Robbins (ed) *Caring for the Dying Patient and the Family*, London: Harper & Row

Copp, L.A. (ed) (1985): *Perspectives on Pain*, Edinburgh: Longman

Corr, C.A. & D.M. Corr (eds) (1985): *Hospice Approaches to Pediatric Care*, New York: Springer Publishing Company

Corr, C.A., I.M. Martinson & K.L. Dyer (1985): 'Parental Bereavement' in Corr & Corr (eds) *op cit*

Culling, J. (1988): 'The Psychological Problems of Families of Children with Cancer' in A. Oakhill (ed) *The Supportive Care of the Child with Cancer*, London: John Wright (Butterworth)

Davies, J. (1979): 'The Parent's Reaction' in P.H. Morris Jones (ed) *Topics in Pediatrics 1: Haematology and Oncology*, Tunbridge Wells: Pitman Medical

Delight, E. & J. Goodall (1988): 'Babies with spina bifida treated without surgery: parents' views on home versus hospital care', *British Medical Journal*, Vol 297, 12 Nov, 1230–33

Department of Health (1986) *Childhood Leukaemia in the Republic of Ireland — Mortality and Incidence*, Dublin: Stationery Office

Dionne, L. (1988): 'La Maison Michel Sarrazin: From Dream to Reality', *Journal of Palliative Care*, 4:3, September

Dominica, F. (1985): 'Helen House: A Hospice for Children' in Corr & Corr (eds) *op cit*

Dominica, F. (1987): 'Reflections on death in childhood', *British Medical Journal*, Vol 294, 10 January, 108–10

Donnelly-Wood, D. (1988): 'Oncology Social Work' in Oakhill (ed) *The Supportive Care of the Child with Cancer*, London: John Wright (Butterworth)

Draper, G.J., J.M. Birch, J.F. Bithell, L.M. Kinnier Wilson, I. Leck, H.B. Marsden, P.H. Morris Jones, C.A. Stiller & R. Swindell (1982): *Childhood Cancer in Britain. Incidence, Survival and Mortality. Studies on medical and population subjects 37*, London: OPCS

Ekert, H. (1983): 'Long term needs of parents and children with life threatening disease', *Australian Family Physician*, Vol 12, no 4, April

Eland, J. (1985a) 'Myths about pain in children', *Candlelighters Childhood Cancer Foundation*, V:1

Eland, J. (1985b): 'The Role of the Nurse in Children's Pain' in L.A. Copp (ed) (1985): *Perspectives on Pain*, Edinburgh, London, Melbourne, New York: Churchill Livingstone

Eland, J. & J. Anderson (1977): 'The Experience of Pain in Children' in A. Jacox (ed) *Pain: A Source Book for Nurses and Other Health Professionals*, Boston: Little Brown

Fagerhaugh S. & A. Strauss (1977): *The Politics of Pain Management*, London etc: Addison Wesley

Fleming, S.J. (1985): 'Children's Grief: Individual and Family Dynamics' in Corr & Corr (eds) *op cit*

Gardner, M.J., M.P. Snee, A.J. Hall, S. Downes, C.A. Powell, J.D. Tennell (1990): 'Results of case-control study of leukaemia and lymphoma among young people near Sellafield nuclear plant in West Cumbria', *British Medical Journal*, 300:423-9

Gath (1989): 'Living with a mentally handicapped brother or sister', *Archives of Disease in Childhood* April, Vol 64, no 4

Gibbons, M.B. (1986): 'When the dying patient is a child: a challenge for the living' in M.J. Hockenberry & D.K. Coody (eds) *Pediatric Oncology and Hematology, Perspectives on Care*, St Louis, Toronto, Princeton: C.V. Mosby

Goodall, J. (1988): 'Learning from the hospice philosophy', *British Journal of Hospital Medicine*, May, 39 (5): 461-2

Gotay, C.C. (1983): 'Models of terminal care: a review of the literature', *Clin Invest Med* (DFG) 6(3):131–41

Graham, P., M. Rutter & S. George (1973): 'Temperamental characteristics of behavior disorders in children', *American Journal of Orthopsychiatry*, 43, 328–39

Gross, S.C. & G.G. Gardner (1980): 'Child Pain: Treatment Approaches' in W.L. Smith, M. Merskey & S. Gross *Pain: Meaning and Management*, Lancaster: MTP

Gyulay, J.E. (1978): *The Dying Child*, New York: McGraw Hill

Hall, D. & M. Stacey (eds) (1979): *Beyond Separation: Further Studies of Children in Hospital*, London: Routledge & Kegan Paul

Harris, A. (1989): 'The Dying Child'. Notes for Workshop on Terminal Care in Children — Symptom Control. St Christopher's Hospice International Conference on Terminal Care

Haslam, D.R. (1969): 'Age and the perception of pain', *Psychonomic Sc*, 15:86

Hinton, J. (1972): *Dying*, Harmondsworth: Penguin

Howarth, R. (1979): 'The child's response to the stress of serious illness' in P.H. Morris Jones (ed) *Topics in Pediatrics 1: Haematology and Oncology*, Tunbridge Wells: Pitman Medical

James, J.A., D. J. Harris, M.G. Mott & A. Oakhill (1988): 'Paediatric oncology information pack for general practitioners', *British Medical Journal* 296: 97–8

Kaiko, R.F. (1980): 'Age and morphine analgesia in cancer patients with post-operative pain', *Clin Pharmacol Rev*, 28: 823–26

Karayalcin, G. (1983): 'Supportive care of child with cancer' in Lanzkowsky (ed) *Pediatric Oncology*, New York: McGraw Hill

Katz, E.R., J. Kellerman & S.E. Siegel (1980): 'Behavioral distress in children with cancer undergoing medical procedures: developmental considerations', *Journal of Consulting and Clinical Psychology*, 48: 356–65

Kazak, A.E. (1989): 'Families of chronically ill children: a systems and social-ecological model of adaptation and challenge', *Journal of Consulting and Clinical Psychology*, Vol 57, No 1, 25-30

Kelly, M. (1989), personal communication

Kendrick C., J. Culling & A. Oakhill (1986): 'Children's understanding of their illness: its treatment within a paediatric oncology unit', *Association of Child Psychology and Psychiatry Newsletter*, Vol 8, 2

Knapp, R.J. (1986): *Beyond Endurance: When a Child Dies*, New York: Schocken Books

Kohler, J.A. & M. Radford (1985): 'Terminal care for children dying of cancer: quantity and quality of life', *British Medical Journal*, 291:115-16

Kramer, R.F. (1984): 'Living with childhood cancer: impact on the healthy siblings', reprinted in Krulik et al (eds) (1987) *The Child and Family Facing Life-threatening Illness*, Philadelphia: Lippincott

Krulik, T., B. Holaday & I.M. Martinson (eds) (1987): *The Child and Family Facing Life-threatening Illness*, Philadelphia: Lippincott

Kubler-Ross, E. (1970): *On Death and Dying*, London: Tavistock Publications

Lamerton, R. (1980): *Care of the Dying*, Harmondsworth: Penguin

Lanskey, S.B., N. Cairns, G. Clark, J. Lowman, L. Miller & R. Trueworthy (1979): 'Childhood cancer: non-medical costs of the illness', *Cancer* 43: 403-08

Lascari, A.D. (1973): *Leukemia in Childhood*, Springfield, Illinois: Charles C. Thomas

Lauer, M. E., R.K. Mulhern, M.J. Schell & B.J. Camitta (1989): 'Long-term follow-up of parental adjustment following a child's death at home or hospital', *Cancer* 63:988-94

Lewis, S., F. T. Horton & S. Armstrong (1987): 'Distress in fatally and chronically ill children: methodological note', in Krulik et al (eds) *op cit*

Bibliography

McDonnell, M.M. (1986): 'Patients' Perceptions of Their Care at Our Lady's Hospice, Dublin', M.Sc. Dissertation (Community Health) Trinity College, Dublin

McGee, M. & M. Fitzgerald (1990): 'Attitudes of urban Irish doctors to the hospitalisation of young children', *Irish Journal of Psychology*, Vol 11, No 1

McGrath, P.A. & L.M. Hillier (1989): 'The enigma of pain in children: an overview', *Pediatrician*, Vol 16, Nos 1-2

McGrath, P.J. & A. Unruh (1987): *Pain in Children and Adolescents*, Amsterdam, New York, London: Elsevier

McWhirter, W.R. & J.P. Masel (1987): *Pediatric Oncology*, Sydney: Williams & Wilkins & Associates

Maguire, P., J. Comaroff, P. Ramsell & P.H. Morris Jones (1979): 'Psychological and Social Problems in Families of Children with Leukaemia' in P.H. Morris Jones (ed) *Topics in Pediatrics 1: Haemotology and Oncology*, Tunbridge Wells: Pitman Medical Publishing

Malpas, J.S. (1979): 'Cancer in Children' in P.H. Morris Jones (ed) *op cit*

Malone, M. M. (1982): 'Consciousness of dying and projective fantasy of young children with malignant disease' reprinted in Krulik et al (1987) (eds) *op cit*

Mann, J. (1989): 'Cancer in Children' in Walsh, T.D. (ed) *Symptom Control*, Oxford: Blackwell Scientific Publications

Marnham, P. (1980): *Lourdes, a Modern Pilgrimage*, London, Toronto, Sydney, New York: Granada

Martin, B. B. (1985): 'Home care for terminally ill children and their families' in Corr & Corr (eds) *op cit*

Martinson, I.M. (1983): *Nursing Times*, March, page 64

Martinson, I.M. (1981): 'The Dying Child' in C. Saunders, D.H. Summers & N. Teller (eds) (1981): *Hospice: the living idea*, London: Arnold

Martinson, I.M. (1987): 'The Feasibility of Home Care for the Dying Child with Cancer' in Krulik et al (eds) *op cit*

Melzack, R. (1987) in Foreword to P.J. McGrath & A. Unruh *Pain in Children and Adolescents*, Amsterdam, New York, London: Elsevier

Melzack, R. & P. Wall (1982): *The Challenge of Pain*, Harmondsworth: Penguin

Miles M.S. & A.S. Demi (1986): 'Guilt in Bereaved Parents' in T.A. Rando (ed) *Parental Loss of a Child*, Illinois: Research Press Company

Miller, R.W. (1988): 'Geographical and Ethnic Differences in the Occurrence of Childhood Cancer' in D.M. Parkin, C.A. Stiller, G.A. Draper, C.A. Bieber, B. Teracini & J.L. Young (eds) (1988): *International Incidence of Childhood Cancer*, Lyon: WHO International Agency for Research on Cancer

Miller, R.W. & F.W. McKay (1984): 'Decline in US childhood cancer mortality', *Journal of American Medical Association*, 251, 1567-70

Miser, A.W., J.A. Dothage, R.A. Wesley & J.S. Miser (1987): 'The prevalence of pain in a pediatric and young adult cancer population', *Pain* 29: 73-83

Miser, A.W., L. Moore, R. Greene et al (1986): 'Prospective study of continuous intravenous and subcutaneous morphine infusions for therapy-related or cancer-related pain in children and young adults with cancer', *Clin J Pain* 2:101-06

Mohide, E.A., J.A. Royle, M. Montemuro, P. Porterfield, J.F. Scott & P.X. Tugwell (1988): 'Assessing the quality of cancer pain management', *Journal of Palliative Care*, 4:3

Monson, R.R. & B. McMahon (1984): 'Pre-natal X-ray exposure and cancer in children' in J.D. Boice & J.F. Fraumeni (eds) *Radiation Carcinogenesis: Epidemiology and Biological Significance*, New York: Raven Press

Mor, V., D.S. Green & R. Kastenbaum (eds) (1988): *The Hospice Experiment*, Baltimore and London: Johns Hopkins University Press

Morris Jones, P.H. (ed) (1979): *Topics in Pediatrics 1: Haematology and Oncology*, Bath: Pitman Medical

Morris Jones, P.H. (1981): 'Current Approaches to Cancer in Childhood' in D. Hull (ed) *Recent Advances in Pediatrics 6*, Edinburgh, London, New York, Melbourne: Churchill Livingstone

Bibliography

Mott, M.G. (1982): 'Caring for children with cancer' in E. Wilkes (ed) *The Dying Patient*, Lancaster: MTP Press, pages 45–56

Mott, M.G. (1990): 'A child with cancer: a family in crisis', *British Medical Journal*, 301:133–4

Murray, K. (1989): 'The Role of the Specialist Nurse in the Home Care Team', *Forum* Vol 5, No 3, March

NESC (National Economic and Social Council) (1987): *Community Care Services: an Overview*, Dublin: NESC

Noordenbos, quoted in 'Prologue' in P. Wall & R. Melzack (eds) (1964) *A Textbook of Pain*, London, Edinburgh, Melbourne, New York: Churchill Livingstone

Oakhill, A. (ed) (1988): *The Supportive Care of the Child with Cancer*, London: John Wright (Butterworth)

O'Connor, S. (1987): *Community Care Services: An Overview*, Dublin: National Economic and Social Council (NESC)

O'Connor, J. & H. Ruddle (1988): *Caring for the Elderly*, Dublin: Stationery Office

Office of Population Censuses and Surveys, (1984): *1982 Mortality Statistics, Childhood* London: HMSO

OPCS Social Survey Division (1985): *A Survey of Recently Bereaved Parents* (unpublished pilot for study not subsequently carried out)

Osterweis, M., F. Solomon & M. Green (eds) (1984): *Bereavement: Reactions, Consequences and Care* (Report by the Committee for the Study of Health Consequences of the Stress of Bereavement, Institute of Medicine, National Academy of Sciences) Washington DC: National Academy Press

Papadatou, D. (1989): 'Caring for dying adolescents', *Nursing Times*, May 3, Vol 85, no 18

Parkes, C.M. (1988): 'Can sophisticated pain and symptom control and psychosocial support be satisfactorily delivered in the home? Not always!' *Journal of Palliative Care* 4:1–2, 50–52

Parkin, D.M., C.A. Stiller, G.J. Draper, C.A. Bieber, B. Teracini & J.L. Young (eds) (1988): *International Incidence of Childhood*

Cancer, Lyon: WHO International Agency for Research on Cancer

Pentol, A. (1982): *The Costs of Childhood Leukaemia and its Treatment*. Working Paper no 67; Health Services Management Unit, Dept. of Social Administration, University of Manchester

Pine, V.R. & C. Brauer (1986): 'Parental grief: a synthesis of theory, research and intervention', in T.A. Rando (ed) *Parental Loss of a Child*, Illinois: Research Press Company

Rana, S.R. (1987): 'Pain — a subject ignored', *Pediatrics*, 79:309–10

Rando, T.A. (1986): 'The unique issues and impact of the death of a child' in Rando (ed) *Parental Loss of a Child*, Illinois: Research Press Company

Rando, T.A. (1988): 'Anticipatory grief: the term is a misnomer but the phenomenon exists', *Journal of Palliative Care*, 4: 1 & 2; 70–73

Robertson, J. (1958): *Young Children in Hospital*, London: Tavistock Publications

Robertson, J. (1962): *Hospitals and Children: A Parent's Eye View*, London: Victor Gollancz

Salvage, J. (1986): *Hospices for Children: A Need in a Sick Society?*, King's Fund report on proceedings of a conference organised jointly by the King's Fund Centre and Helen House Hospice for Children

Sanders, C.M. (1980): 'A comparison of adult bereavement in the death of a spouse, child and parent', *Omega*, 10, 303–21

Saunders, C. (ed) (1978): *The Management of Terminal Disease*, London: Edward Arnold

Saunders, C., D. Summers & N. Teller (eds) (1981a): *Hospice: the Living Idea*. London: Edward Arnold

Saunders, C. (1981b): 'Current views on pain research and terminal care', in Swerdlow, M. (ed) *The Therapy of Pain*, Lancaster: MTP Press

Saunders, C. (1989) in closing address to St Christopher's Fifth International Conference on Hospice, London. Audio Bass tape

Bibliography

Schechter, N.L., D.A. Allen & K. Hanson (1986): 'Status of pediatric pain control: a comparison of hospital analgesic usage in children and adults', *Pediatrics*, Vol 77, No 1, January

Schiff, H. (1977): *The Bereaved Parent*, New York: Crown

Schmidt, L. (1987): 'Working with bereaved parents' in Krulik et al (eds) op cit

Sherman, M. (1981): *The Leukaemic Child*, USA: National Institutes of Health publication No 81–863

Spinetta, J., D. Rigler & M. Karon (1973): 'Anxiety in the dying child', *Pediatrics* 52:841

Stacey, M. (ed) R. Dearden, R. Pill & D. Robinson (1970): *Hospitals, Children and their Families*, London: Routledge & Kegan Paul

Stein, A., G.C. Forrest, H. Woolley & J.D. Baum (1989): 'Life threatening illness and hospice care', *Arch Dis Ch*, Vol 64, 697–702

Stenbak, E. (1986): *Care of Children in Hospital*, Copenhagen: WHO

Stephenson, J. (1986): 'Grief of siblings' in T.A. Rando (ed) *Parental Loss of a Child*, Illinois: Research Press Company

Stoddard, S. (1978): *Hospice Movement — A Better Way of Caring for the Dying*, New York: Stein and Day

Swafford, L.I. & D. Allen (1968): 'Pain relief in the pediatric patient', *Medical Clinics of North America*, 48: 131–3

Swerdlow, M. & V. Ventafridda (eds) (1987) *Cancer Pain*, Lancaster: MTP, pp 3–7

Tebbi, C.K. (ed) (1987): *Major Topics in Adolescent Oncology*, New York: Future Publishing Co

Thomas, A., S. Chess & H.G. Birch (1968): *Temperament and Behavior Disorder in Children*, New York: New York University Press

Thornes, R. (1988): *Care of Dying Children and Their Families*, Birmingham: National Association of Health Authorities

Tietz W., L. McSherry & B. Britt (1977): 'Family sequelae after a child's death due to cancer', *American Journal of Psychotherapy* 26 (3): 417–25

Twycross, R. & S. Lack (1983): *Symptom Control in Far Advanced Cancer*, London: Pitman

Twycross, R. & S. Lack (1984): *Therapeutics in Terminal Cancer*, London: Pitman

Varni, J.W., G.A. Walco & E.R. Katz (1989): 'Assessment and Management of Chronic and Recurrent Pain in Children with Chronic Diseases', *Pediatrician*, Vol 16, No 1-2

Ventafridda, V. & M. Swerdlow (1984) p 161 in E. Wilkes & J. Levy (eds): *Advances in Morphine Therapy*, London: Royal Society of Medicine

Vere, D. (1984) p 127 in E. Wilkes & J. Levy (eds): *Advances in Morphine Therapy*, London: Royal Society of Medicine

Waechter, E. (1964): 'Death, dying and bereavement: a review of the literature' reprinted in Krulik et al (eds) *op cit*

Waechter, E. (1971): 'Children's awareness of fatal illness', reprinted in Krulik et al (eds) *op cit*

Waechter, E. (1972): 'Children's reactions to fatal illness' reprinted in Krulik et al (1987) *op cit*

Waechter, E. (1979): 'The Adolescent with Chronic Life-threatening Illness' reprinted in Krulik et al (eds) *op cit*

Waechter, E. (1983): 'Dying Children: Patterns of Coping' reprinted in Krulik et al (eds) *op cit*

Walker, A. (ed) (1982): *Community Care: The Family, the State and Social Policy*, Oxford: Basil Blackwell and Martin Robertson

Wall, P. & R. Melzack (eds) (1984): *Textbook of Pain*, Edinburgh, London, Melbourne, New York: Churchill Livingstone

Walsh, T.D. (1985): 'Common misunderstandings about the use of morphine for chronic pain in advanced cancer', *CA — A Cancer Journal for Clinicians*, Vol 35, no 3

Ward, P. & A. Oakhill (1988): 'Terminal Care' in A. Oakhill (ed) *The Supportive Care of the Child with Cancer*, London: John Wright (Butterworth)

Weiss, R.S. (1988): 'Is it possible to prepare for trauma?' *Journal of Palliative Care*, 4: 1 & 2

West, R. (1984): 'Childhood cancer mortality: international comparisons 1955-74', *World Health Stat Q.*, 37, 98-127

Bibliography

Wheeler, P.W., N.F. Lange & S.J. Bertolone (1985): 'Improving care for hospitalized terminally ill children: a practicable model' in Corr & Corr (eds) *Hospice Approaches to Pediatric Care*, New York: Springer Publishing Company

WHO (1986): *Cancer Pain Relief*, Geneva: WHO

Wilkes, E. (1980): *Report of the Working Group on Terminal Care Standing Medical Advisory Committee*. London: Department of Health and Social Security

Wilkes, E. (1986): 'Introduction' to Wilkes, E. (ed) *Terminal Care*, Guildford: Update Siebert Publications

Wilkes, E. & J. Levy (eds) (1984): *Advances in Morphine Therapy: 1983 International Symposium on Pain Control*, London: Royal Society of Medicine

Williamson, P.S. & M.L. Williamson (1983): 'Physiologic stress reduction by a local anaesthetic during newborn circumcision', *Pediatrics*, 71:36–40

Wilson, D. (1985): 'Developing a hospice program for children' in Corr & Corr (eds) *Hospice Approaches to Pediatric Care*, New York: Springer Publishing Company

Woolley, H., A. Stein, G.C. Forrest & J.D. Baum (1989): 'Imparting the diagnosis of life threatening illness in children', *British Medical Journal*, 298:1623–26

Zeltzer, L.K. (1989): Introduction to *Pediatrician*, Vol 16, Nos 1–2

Zeltzer, L.K. & P.M. Zeltzer (1989): 'Clinical assessment and pharmacologic treatment of pain in children: cancer as the model for the management of chronic or persistent pain', *Pediatrician*, Vol 16, No 1–2

Zevon, M.A., C.A. Tebbi & M. Stern (1987): 'Psychological and familiar factors in adolescent oncology' in C.K.Tebbi (ed) *Major Topics in Adolescent Oncology*, New York: Future Publishing Co

Zimmerman, J. (ed) (1986): *Hospice*, Baltimore and Munchen: Urban & Schwarzenberg

Zorza, R. and Zorza, V. (1980): *A Way to Die*, London: André Deutsch

Index

A
adolescents
  boredom, 70-2
  hospital care for, 28, 48-9
  special needs of, 12-13
  terminal care of, 91
amputation, 28, 33, 35, 48, 77
  artificial limbs, 71
anaesthesia
  not used for children, 38, 101
Atavan, 116

B
Bluebond-Langner, M., 118
bone-marrow transplants, 28, 38-40, 106
boredom, 70-2
Britain, treatment in, 28-9, 50, 58
Broviac, 54-5

C
Calpol, 103
cancer
  appearance of health, 59-60
  causes of, 11-12
  curable types, 12, 25
  diagnosis of, 16-22
  effects on families, 59-72
  rate of among children, 11
  relapses, 85-6
  treatment of, 23-6
chemotherapy, 35, 38, 39, 48-9, 86
  isolation from infection, 53
  mis-timing, 56
communication
  difficulties of, 46, 47, 86-7
  with dying children, 117-25
  importance of, 31-7
community support, 73-84
  visitors, 83-4
consultants
  communication with parents, 17, 31-7, 45-7
  and home care, 93, 104-5, 107
counselling
  need for, 34-5, 64
  and treatment decisions, 39

D
death
  discussion of, 117-25
  grieving after, 128-37
  last days, 117-27
  last hours, 125-7
  living with bereavement, 131-4
  preparation for, 89-90
decision-making
  and information, 37-41
depression, 53-4
diagnosis, 16-22
  acceptance of, 87-8
  communication of, 17, 20-1
  parents' reactions to, 18-20, 21-2
  symptoms, 16-18
  of terminal illness, 27(t), 85-7
doctors, 42-3, 71, 126, 129
  communication of diagnosis, 16-21, 86-7
  communication with children, 122-3, 125
  communication with parents, 30-7
  difficulties with, 45-7, 54-7
  and home care, 94, 102-4, 107, 113, 114-15
  and medical costs, 76
  and predictions of death, 117-18
Domiciliary Care Allowance, 77-8
Down's Syndrome, 40, 69
Dublin Corporation, 72

F
faith-healer, 81
families
  effects of grief, 135-6
  effects of illness, 59-72
  involvement of siblings, 65-8
  strains of hospitalisation, 51-2
  stresses within, 61-5
  support systems for, 28
financial problems, 52, 61-2, 73-5
  expenses, 74-5
  medical costs, 76-7
fund-raising, 73, 75, 78-9
funeral arrangements, 89-90

Index

G
Gaelic Athletic Association (GAA), 79
grief, 128-37
  living with bereavement, 131-4

H
health services, 76-8
  assessment of, 96-8
Hinton, J., 118, 119
  home care, 91-8, 113-15
  isolation, 98
  and pain control, 102-7
home help services, 78
hospice movement, 12, 40, 88, 93, 96, 112-13, 118
  home care, 103-4, 109, 115
  and hospitals, 111
hospital care
  adapting to hospitalisation, 53-4
  for adolescents, 28, 48-9
  ancillary staff, 57
  cancer wards, 42-3, 50-1, 58
  chaplains, 81
  facilitation of parents, 49-52
  facilities, 56-8
  negative aspects, 44-8
  and pain control, 107-9, 111-16
  quality of, 42-8, 54-6
  treatment of children, 28-9
hospitals
  terminal care in, 93-4

I
information
  and decision-making, 37-41
  lack of literature, 32, 36
  need for, 30-7
Irish Cancer Society, 77
Irish Council for the Blind, 70-1
Irish Wheelchair Association, 71
irradiation treatment, 28, 38

K
Knock shrine, 80

L
leukaemia, 11, 12, 69
  relapses, 36, 86
  transplants, 28, 38-40, 106

Lions' Club, 77
Lourdes shrine, 60, 78-9, 85, 110

M
Manchester Children's Tumour Registry, 11
Melzack, R., 101
morphine, 99-100
  syringe driver, 109, 115-16
  in terminal care, 102-16
Murray, Kathleen, 98

N
needles, fear of, 54-5
nurses, 34, 43, 45-6, 77
  comments on, 55-6
  and home care, 94-6

O
Omnopon, 106, 111
opiates, 99-100

P
pain
  caused by treatment, 25
  in children, 101-2
  degrees of, 100-2
  delays in alleviation, 45
  moderate to mild, controlled, 102-3
  moderate to severe, mostly controlled, 103-5
  severe, out of control at times, 105-16
  symptom control, 17, 98, 99-116
parents
  exhaustion of, 61
  facing terminal diagnosis, 85-7
  fear of marriage breakdown, 62-3
  financial problems, 52, 61-2, 73-5
  grief after bereavement, 128-37
  and home care, 91-2
  hospital facilitation of, 42, 49-52, 56-8
  interviews with, 13-15
  need for information, 30-7
  pregnancies, 64-5
  preparing for death, 117-25
  reactions to diagnosis, 18-20, 21-2
  sense of despair, 60

'special child', 64, 134-6
tensions between, 52, 63-4
unable to ease pain, 25
Parkes, Colin Murray, 92
pharmacists, 96, 104
pilgrimages, 78-80, 110
Ponstan, 17, 103, 104, 108, 110, 111
pregnancies, 65-6
priests, 80-1
psychiatric treatment, 53-4
psychogenic pain, 100-2
public health nurses, 71, 78, 93, 126
and home care, 94-5, 102-4, 107, 114

R
religion, support of, 78-81

S
Saunders, Cicely, 91
school attendance, 68-70, 107
social workers, 34
and allowances, 77-8
and preparations for death, 89-90
specialist units, 42-3, 44, 48, 50, 82
and home care, 93
and terminal diagnosis, 86-7
unrelieved pain, 110-12
steroids, 23, 74, 110
surgery
described as 'successful', 33, 35
symptom control. see pain
syringe driver, 109, 115-16

T
terminal care, 12-13, 85-98
development of, 12-13
at home, 91-3
in hospitals, 93-4
last days, 117-27
preparations for death, 89-90
worsening symptoms, 90, 102
transport problems, 73-4, 78
treatment, 23-6
costs of, 76-7
decisions on continuing, 37-41
for families, 28
sensitisation to pain, 102
treatment centres, 26-9, 43
and home care, 93
and pain control, 108-9
Twycross, R. and Lack, S., 117

U
United States of America, 90

V
Voluntary Health Insurance Scheme (VHI), 76

W
wheelchairs, 71-2